Stammering

What is stammering? How does it present itself? When does it occur? Why does it happen? What are the most effective strategies you can use to help?

Providing background information about stammering as well as a wide range of tools and strategies, this practical book is for teachers, student teachers, SENCOs, parents and anyone else concerned about children in their care who present with stammering.

Full of tips and advice, the book has separate sections on early years, primary and secondary levels. It covers the most common areas that teachers must consider when supporting children who lack speech fluency, including:

- identifying children at risk of developing a stammer
- how to manage incidents of stammering
- how to manage classroom communication and oral participation
- helping children to make and maintain relationships
- helping children to manage feelings associated with stammering
- working alongside speech and language therapists.

Recent changes to the curriculum mean that there is now a greater demand than ever on children's communication skills. This accessible book will help adults provide the necessary support to children who stammer by offering a clear explanation of the presentation of stammering and the best ways to manage occurrences of stammering in a range of school contexts.

Trudy Stewart is a retired consultant speech and language therapist who has written and researched extensively on stammering in children and adults.

Stammering

A resource book for teachers

Trudy Stewart

Routledge
Taylor & Francis Group

LONDON AND NEW YORK

First published 2016
by Routledge
2 Park Square, Milton Park, Abingdon, Oxon, OX14 4RN

and by Routledge
711 Third Avenue, New York, NY 10017

Routledge is an imprint of the Taylor & Francis Group, an informa business

British Library Cataloguing in Publication Data
A catalogue record for this book is available from the British Library

Library of Congress Cataloging in Publication Data
Names: Stewart, Trudy, author.
Title: Stammering : a resource book for teachers / Trudy Stewart.
Description: New York, NY : Routledge, 2016. | Includes bibliographical
references and index.
Identifiers: LCCN 2015046314 | ISBN 9781138936287 (hardback : alk. paper) |
ISBN 9781138936300 (pbk. : alk. paper) | ISBN 9781315676920 (ebook)
Subjects: LCSH: Stuttering in children. | Speech therapy for children. |
Language arts. | Children with mental disabilities–Language. | Teachers
of children with disabilities.
Classification: LCC LC4028 .S74 2016 | DDC 371.91/4–dc23LC
record available at http://lccn.loc.gov/2015046314

ISBN: 978-1-138-93628-7 (hbk)
ISBN: 978-1-138-93630-0 (pbk)
ISBN: 978-1-315-67692-0 (ebk)

Typeset in Bembo
by Keystroke, Station Road, Codsall, Wolverhampton
Printed and bound in Great Britain by
Ashford Colour Press Ltd, Gosport, Hampshire

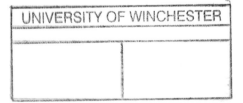

Dedication

To all teachers who work collaboratively with pupils who stammer, making school life that bit easier.

Contents

Acknowledgements

My grateful thanks go to Messrs P. Lambert, P. Maud and F. Lyden, and Ms J. Brocklebank who shared their experience and expertise and gave me invaluable advice on current educational practices.

Thanks also to speech and language colleagues past and present, Jackie Turnbull, Jo Holmes and Claire Bull, who read early drafts and were kind in their feedback and comments.

Finally to all teachers and pupils who I visited in schools and from whom I learnt so much.

Introduction

Stammering is a disorder of speech which is frequently misunderstood – misunderstood by employers, teachers, parents, peers and even by the individual himself. (The majority of people who stammer are male, so this book uses the male pronoun throughout. Similarly, for teachers and speech and language therapists, the book uses the female pronoun.) No wonder it is difficult to manage when there is often misleading and conflicting advice.

Stammering needs to be understood as more than a speech problem, rather as a communication disorder with the potential to affect all aspects of a child's life: his relationships, career choices, education and view of himself. When those around the child have that understanding, research has shown they also have better, more desirable attitudes towards stammering and the individual affected (Crowe & Walton, 1981).

Stammering may be resolved if it is managed early, and in the absence of compounding issues. In some cases stammering may persist but can be limited in it's development. It's impact on the individual's communication, his feelings and thoughts about himself and the way he is able to live his life need not be compromised. The goals of management may change as the pupil matures but as Reardon-Reeves and Yaruss (2013, p. 211) write:

> Rather than focusing on a largely unattainable goal of 'perfect' or 'normal' fluency, we seek to help the child learn to communicate effectively with increased fluency, decreased tension, reduced negative reactions, minimal impact of stuttering and an environment that is both supportive and accepting.

At various points in his life each individual child who stammers will need to learn to manage his stammer. This will mean facing fears and anxieties and taking risks. Those who are most successful in meeting these challenges are those with courage, inner resilience and a degree of creativity. Pupils rarely arrive at school with these characteristics and teachers play an important role in helping individuals find and develop these aspects of themselves.

This book is written for teachers and others working directly with those who stammer. Chapters 1 and 2 provide general information on what stammering is, how it develops and the factors which can maintain it into adulthood. These chapters are useful for anyone working with a dysfluent individual as they provide the necessary information to understand the nature and occurrence of stammering in children and young people.

The majority of the remainder of the book (Chapters 3–7) is divided up into preschool, primary and secondary chapters. Teachers may focus on the sections which are relevant for them. However, the other chapters may be useful in providing a context for the child's stammer, with specific information included in them on how the stammer developed and what issues the pupil has faced or may face in the future.

Throughout the book there are stories of individuals who stammer. These are real stories and clearly illustrate the effect stammering had on their experience of the education system. Perhaps these examples will prove to be the most useful parts of the book. For my part, I have learnt most from listening to the narratives of those who stammer and trying to understand their experience from their perspective.

In the final section of the book (Chapter 8), I have included information on how a speech and language therapist might work alongside school staff. I believe that professional collaboration is one of the keys to helping an individual identify, make and maintain the necessary changes.

During my years of working with those who stammer I have had the privilege to work with numerous teachers who have helped pupils to reach their potential. There have been others who just did not know how to help and were keen to find the 'right way' to manage stammering. It is my wish that this book will meet the needs of this latter group and others who are looking for information. I hope it will lead to greater clarity about what is required and what can make a difference for a pupil who stammers.

1 Stammering

Background information

Kyle is a three-year-old boy who repeats the first sound of each sentence, mainly when he talks to his Gran. She asks him lots of questions and he finds it hard to think of the answers in the time she gives him to answer.

Sophie is in primary school. Her stammer has changed over time and now sounds more like sounds being stretched or prolonged. She sometimes hits her leg to make the sound stop. In school she is finding it hard to cope with situations such as reading aloud and speaking out in front of the class.

Raj is a teenager and attends a large secondary school. You rarely hear him stammer and in class he speaks very little. When he does speak out he uses lots of strategies to avoid stammering, such as switching words, rearranging his sentences and pretending he has forgotten what he wants to say.

Introduction

In this opening chapter, background information on stammering as a speech disorder will be presented: the what, when and why of stammering, factors which can influence fluency and myths associated with stammering.

It is important for teachers to be able to identify specific examples of stammering in children, so there are sections on how stammering presents and the differences between stammering and other disruptions occurring in everyday speech.

The chapter also includes information on the implications of stammering and the consequences for the individual who stammers over a long period of time. These consequences can be physical, emotional and psychological responses which impact on the individual. In order to demonstrate these effects, some examples of adults who stammer will be included in this chapter.

At some point in their lives, 5 per cent of the general population will stammer. This falls to 1 per cent in adults, indicating that many spontaneously recover from the experience. However, determining which individual is likely to recover is not straightforward.

What is stammering?

Defining fluency

'Fluency' is a term that can be applied to speech and relates to the flow and timing of the production of language. Speakers can have varying degrees of fluency, with some individuals demonstrating slower, more hesitant speech.

Differences between stammering and normal disruptions in speaking

All of us experience disruptions in the fluency of our speech, especially children who are learning to speak and developing mature language forms. It is important to differentiate these normal disruptions from stammering. Normal interruptions to fluency include:

- phrase repetitions (*I want, I want a biscuit*)
- interjections (*What time is, er, the kick off?*)
- silent pauses (*. . . I don't know the answer*)
- hesitations (*I think it's a kind of . . . food*)
- some word repetitions (*It's, it's so unfair*).

Stammering is a speech disorder in which the flow or fluency of speaking is disrupted. In some countries, such as the United States and Australia, it is called 'stuttering' but this refers to the same disorder.

   The interruptions which characterise stammering often occur at the beginning of utterances, but can also happen on words which carry most meaning in the sentence, such as nouns and verbs. The disruptions tend to be of two main types:

- repetitions of sounds (*C-c-c-can I go now?*) or syllables (*I like bu-bu-burgers*) or monosyllabic words (*My sister is is is in that class*)
- moments when the articulation of a sound appears to have frozen – this can result in sound prolongation, e.g. *sssssock*, or alternatively the sound is stopped at the larynx (voice box), resulting in no sound being made and the speaker appearing to be stuck or blocked.

Other behaviours occurring with stammering

While attempting to control stammering, an individual can develop other behaviours such as:

- disrupted breathing where too much or too little air is taken in – when a speaker tries to speak on too little air or is unable to control his exhaled air effectively
- issues with rate of speech – a speaker will speed up his talking during a period of fluent speech or slow it down when a difficult word is anticipated
- tense production of sounds – a person puts more effort into his articulation of sounds resulting in forced or 'pushed' articulation

- attempts to minimise the impact of or reduce and/or speed up the disruption – the kinds of strategies usually employed involve the speaker putting more effort into talking. In so doing he can show struggle and tension in speech muscles or other parts of the body (e.g. in his shoulders or stomach) and make unusual movements such as facial distortions, tics and/or movement of the limbs.

Avoidance associated with stammering

A person who stammers often develops an aversion and sensitivity to the stammering itself and tries to avoid doing it. The avoidance may take a number of forms.

- **Word avoidance** – he might avoid saying a word that he stammers on by switching the word and replacing it with a word with a similar meaning. If no similar word is available, he may replace the feared word with a totally different one. This could change the meaning of his sentence but he will regard this as preferable to openly stammering.
- **Situation avoidance** – in these instances the individual will avoid placing himself in communication situations in which he fears stammering. Children and young people report avoiding situations in which they have to say their name, read aloud, speak in front of groups or ask for items in shops. (Examples for adults who stammer include making introductions, ordering in restaurants or bars, asking for specific items in shops and asking for a ticket on a bus, train or at the cinema or theatre.)
- **Relationship avoidance** – a person who stammers may be socially isolated because he avoids groups, making and receiving phone calls, or engaging in simple conversations which help to maintain relationships with others.
- **Feeling avoidance** – an individual might avoid expressing his feelings because he stammers in situations where he feels strong emotions. This can include expressing anger or affection, apologising or saying 'thank you'.

Over time these avoidance behaviours become part of the stammering itself and compound the difficulties with speech.

The impact of stammering

Stammering is regarded as a speech disorder, but this is not the whole story. Communication is such an important part of life: it plays a major role in the development of relationships and how we portray ourselves to others. Compromising communication can lead to difficulty with relationships, educational and career choices, and fundamentally the way people understand themselves. (There will be more information on this in Chapter 2 on how stammering develops.)

> *Brian referred himself to a speech and language therapist as an adult. He had spent a lifetime avoiding stammering: when growing up, in school, in university and now in his workplace. He had ended up choosing not to study the subjects he was best at because they involved giving presentations to his peer group.*
>
> *As a result, Brian was in a career path that was not satisfying. He was socially isolated and unable to ask the woman he liked to go out with him. Stammering had been a major influence in defining the life he was leading. Now he had had enough and wanted to live a different life.*

When does stammering start?

Stammering in children

Stammering tends to start between the ages of 2 and 5, often around 3½. This coincides with the time of significant language development in children. There are incidences of stammering starting later, in primary school years and in teenagers; however, these are much less common.

Stammering in adults

Stammering may also begin in adulthood but again it is much less common. This is referred to as 'acquired stammering' and differs significantly from that which occurs in children. It's onset at this time often relates to issues unconnected with development, such as neurological or progressive degenerative conditions, side effects of medicines, trauma or stressful incidents.

Variability

Variability is one of the most challenging issues surrounding stammering. A person who stammers will report his speech fluency changing within a day, and from day to day, as he experiences different speaking demands, different listeners, and feels more or less tired, or more or less confident.

In addition, the stammer can seem to have a life of its own, with a speaker being aware of a cyclical pattern to it's presentation over time. For example, he may be aware of speaking with greater fluency over a period of months and then perceive a gradual but significant dip over several weeks.

There are a number of well-documented factors affecting variability, some having a positive effect and others a less helpful outcome.

Factors that have a positive effect

It should be noted that while these factors can all improve fluency, not all of them could be used therapeutically to help a child speak more fluently.

NOVELTY

When a speaker puts on a different way of talking, perhaps using a regional accent, a 'funny' voice with a higher/lower pitch, or a change in the rate or volume of speech, the result can be a short-term increase of fluency. This will only last while the new way of speaking is used but once it is habituated, and is no longer novel, the benefits will cease.

TALKING WHEN ALONE, TALKING TO YOUNG CHILDREN AND ANIMALS

In all of these situations a person who stammers will find his dysfluency significantly decreases and in many cases disappears altogether. It is unclear why this happens but it is suggested by experts that it relates to communication demand. In all of these situations there is little or no demand on the person who is speaking: he is usually the person who initiates and controls the interaction, and the level of language required is not demanding.

SINGING

Generally, children and adults who stammer are fluent when they sing. This can be puzzling to the general public who may misinterpret the stammering as something that can be controlled using singing, i.e. 'Just sing what you want to say.' What we know about singing is that it is different from speaking in a number of ways: it uses different parts of the brain, a melody is dictated, words are usually provided and it is not interactive (i.e. does not involve spontaneous turn taking). All of these factors usually play a part in establishing fluency in speech.

LISTENING TO WHITE NOISE OR A DISTRACTING SOUND THROUGH HEADPHONES

This effect has been observed in children and adults. It has formed the basis of some technical aids to fluency since the 1960s, and more recently mobile apps can be purchased to perform the same function. One such example featured in the television programme *Educating Yorkshire* in 2014: a pupil was encouraged to wear headphones which played music while reading and speaking out. This produced a dramatic increase in his ability to speak fluently. Again it is unclear why this affects fluency but the benefits are limited: it can only be used in certain situations and many people 'override' the stimulus, learning to ignore the distracting sound over time.

READING ALONGSIDE ANOTHER PERSON AND/OR READING/SPEAKING IMMEDIATELY AFTER ANOTHER PERSON

Children who stammer can speak more fluently when speaking at the same time or slightly behind another. Experts believe that this corrects some deficit in the auditory pathway of the person who stammers. It can be used as a helpful strategy in some performance-type situations. Beyond this, it has limited usefulness.

ADAPTATION

This technical term relates to a phenomenon observed when an individual who stammers reads the same passage three or four times. The frequency of the stammering decreases at each reading. However, the effect stops if the exercise is prolonged.

ADJACENCY

A second phenomenon relating to reading is one in which a person is asked to read a passage and the occurrence of stammers is noted. The stammered words are removed from the passage and the person is asked to read the altered passage. Stammering will be observed to occur on the words which are adjacent to those which have been removed. This may be a feature of the reader's anticipation of stammering at the same points in the reading.

RELAXATION

The positive effect of physical and mental relaxation is frequently reported by individuals who stammer. This can be naturally occurring relaxation attained through leisure activities or induced through specific relaxation exercises. Meditation and mindfulness practices can also help create a more relaxed state of mind. Some people also report a relaxed effect from drinking certain amounts of alcohol but this is lost if the amount drunk is excessive.

Factors that have a negative effect

These factors are not particularly unusual or surprising as many fluent speakers will experience similar negative effects on their fluency.

TIME PRESSURE

A speaker will increase his rate of speech if he perceives he has limited time to speak or is speaking to a person with a naturally fast rate of speech. This increase can often result in loss of control of speech fluency. It may be due to a lack of preparation or processing before speech, inaccurate messages to the speech muscles, or may be due to the muscles' inability to work accurately above certain speeds.

COMMUNICATION PRESSURE

There are certain situations which demand more of a speaker in terms of the language used, the interactive skills required and the importance the speaker gives the situation. These include interviews, getting married, giving presentations or other situations involving speaking in front of others who may be perceived as judging communication.

PHYSICAL STATE

A speaker who is feeling tired, unwell or upset will be less able to exert the required effort to control his speech. Similarly, fluent speech can be compromised if a person's physical state is undermined by excessive alcohol, drug use or stress-related issues.

LINGUISTIC FACTORS

There are a number of factors which make stammering more likely to occur:

- specific sounds or words at the beginning of an utterance
- longer, more grammatically complex utterances
- longer words.

There is also evidence to suggest that children whose language skills are already compromised, for example those with phonological (i.e. sound-production) difficulties or those with delayed language development, are at risk of chronic stammering.

Why does stammering occur?

Historically, research has failed to identify one specific factor that results in the occurrence of dysfluent speech in children. If you looked at all the current literature on stammering, you would struggle to find a single cause of stammering upon which experts agree.

Current theories relate the cause of stammering to a number of factors that interact and make stammering more likely to happen. These factors include:

- **issues inherent in the child** himself, such as his language development and temperament
- **factors within his environment**, such as the level of difficulty or 'demand' of the communication context in which he speaks and any time pressure on his speaking.

(Significant factors which place a child at risk of developing chronic stammering will be discussed in Chapter 2.)

In trying to identify a cause for stammering, there are interesting findings in the area of the brain and it's functions. Recent research studies comparing fluent and dysfluent speakers have shown differences in the brain function and the areas of the brain which are active during speech. While these recent developments may not directly affect how we manage stammering in schools, the other factors which compound the problem, such as environmental issues, can be effectively managed and are relevant to teachers and their classrooms.

Stammering myths

Finally in this chapter, let's look at some of the common myths around stammering.

Myth 1: Children and adults who stammer do so because they are nervous or lack confidence

There is no evidence to support this statement. In fact, the research demonstrates that those individuals who stammer show the same range of personality features as would an average population. So we are no more and no less likely to meet a person who stammers with low self-esteem than we are to meet a fluent speaker with poor self-confidence.

Myth 2: Children and adults who stammer are less intelligent than the average person

Once again, the research indicates that this statement holds no validity. As a group, people who stammer show the same range of intelligence as the general population.

Myth 3: Stammering has a physical cause

Children and adults who stammer have normal speech anatomy and musculature. Occasionally there may be some minor coordination issues with tongue or lip movements, but this can usually be rectified by appropriate exercises. As has been discussed earlier in this chapter, the more likely cause of stammering is now thought to be related to differences in neurophysiology, compounded by genetic and other issues.

Myth 4: Stammering is caused by a traumatic event

On occasions parents may link the onset of stammering in their child with a single incident. These may be simple events such as an illness or the loss of a toy, or may be highly significant in the life of the family such as the death of a loved one or a physical accident.

While these events are important in the family, a single incident would rarely have a correlation with development of speech fluency. What may happen is that the child has been speaking in that way for some time, then the carer or significant other person recognises the child's dysfluent speech at the same time as the specific incident or event takes place and creates a link in their own mind.

Another explanation for the link between an event and the occurrence of stammering is that the child was struggling to managing his speech but then an event tips the balance and he is no longer able to control his talking.

With regard to adults the situation is somewhat different. As stated earlier on in this chapter on page 4, stammering *can* be acquired in adulthood as a result of trauma and/ or stress, but this is relatively unusual.

Myth 5: Stammering is contagious

Stammering is not a disease that is transmitted from person to person. Children do not 'catch' stammering by mixing with other children who stammer, hearing or copying their dysfluent speech. (As we will see in Chapter 2, lots of children experience dysfluency in preschool years so it is unsurprising that children in the same class will start to stammer at the same time.)

Myth 6: Stammering is a deliberate way of talking

Some people believe that stammering is something a person does on purpose, a deliberate act which has some benefit, for example getting the child out of an activity or speaking situation. The implication of this belief is that the child is able to change the way he speaks at will and can choose to speak more fluently.

In fact, the consequences of stammering are not pleasant or attractive and those who see benefits to dysfluent speech are not aware of the full impact of the disorder. Once established, stammering is very difficult to change and a child does not have the control to modify the fluency of his speech at will.

Key points to remember

- Children who stammer do so in many different ways.
- Stammering is a highly variable disorder.
- A child who stammers will experience different levels of fluency within the course of a day, across different situations, and with different people.
- What you see is not always what you get. Not all stammering is obvious: some less-obvious behaviours result from the individual's attempts to hide his stammer.
- It is not enough to manage the observable stammering: the emotional and cognitive impact must also be of concern to those trying to help the child.

2 The development of stammering in young children

Jack is a bright and lively 3 year old who is repeating words at the beginning of sentences. He seems unaware of this behaviour but it has been noticed by his family. His mother and grandmother both stammer but react to Jack's speech in different ways. His mother appears interested in the content of his communication rather than how he speaks.

Gran, however, is more critical and advises Jack to modify his speech when he is dysfluent. She tells him at various times to 'stop', 'speak slowly', 'think before you speak', 'just relax', 'take your time', 'spit it out' or 'hurry up'.

Jack is learning that Gran is more difficult to talk to. He is beginning to feel that he can't talk properly to her but is not sure exactly what he is doing wrong.

Introduction

It is important for teachers to be aware of how stammering develops. If the factors that indicate persistent stammering are identified early in a child it increases the likelihood of a positive outcome. So this chapter will describe in detail what is understood currently about the development of stammering in childhood and the factors which indicate that a child is at risk of developing a persistent stammer.

The chapter concludes with a description of a model which has been applied to the development of stammering in children. The model is called the demand and capacities model and brings together much of the research findings about early stammering and helps explain its variability.

When does stammering start?

While a small number of children appear to be dysfluent from starting to speak, most experience the onset of stammering between the ages of 2 and 5. The third year of life appears to be very important in the development of a child's fluency. The greatest risk of the onset of stammering occurs before 3 years, with 75 per cent occurring before 3½ years. Consequently, professionals in preschool education settings can play an important role in helping to identify the early signs of stammering in children.

How does stammering develop and resolve?

At the start

When a young child first begins to experience dysfluent speech it may be quite severe. Some parents report their child as being 'unable to get a word out'. Understandably, this can worry parents and carers but it is generally not significant in relation to the level of stammering in later life. Research has shown that this initial level is not related to how dysfluent the child may be as a teenager or adult.

Changes in the first 2–3 years of stammering

Most children show recovery in the first 14 months following the onset of stammering. Boys, however, take longer to recover than girls; according to research, their recovery can last between 24–36 months, while girls will take between 12–18 months. For these improving children the pattern of recovery will be variable; the level of fluency will be up and down but will show an improving trend over time. However, children who are likely to have a persistent stammer show less variability in speech fluency and do not demonstrate the overall improving trend; their fluency levels seem to plateau after 12 months.

Who is likely to develop stammering?

Risk factors

In recent years, researchers have identified a number of risk factors that make the development of stammering more likely in some children. These factors are described in detail below.

Gender

Boys are more likely to stammer than girls. The ratio is about 4:1. The reasons for this are not widely understood but it is interesting to note that boys develop many language skills more slowly than girls.

As mentioned earlier in this chapter, there are marked differences in how boys and girls recover from early dysfluent speech. According to research, boys' recovery from dysfluent speech is also slower than girls and can take up to three years.

The following case study is typical of the recovery pattern that many girls show.

> *Rebecca's mum noticed her start to stammer when she was around 3 years old. The stammer consisted mainly of sound and whole-word repetitions and could happen at any time when she spoke, i.e. at the beginning or in the middle of utterances. It did not seem to follow any particular pattern but would come and go over a period of several weeks.*
>
> *Rebecca's mum contacted a speech and language therapist and together they monitored and observed her talking on a regular basis. On several occasions they both concluded that her speech needed some direct work, but each time it improved before the sessions started.*

By the time Rebecca was 4½ years old, the dysfluencies had all but disappeared and neither her mum nor the therapist were concerned. Throughout all that time, Rebecca appeared unaware of the disruptions in her speech and continued to communicate without concern.

Genetics

A child who has a parent or close family member who stammers or who has stammered at some point in the past is more at risk of developing a stammer. Research also indicates that a child can inherit the 'recovery' gene: if the family member stammered as a child but does not stammer as an adult, then the child is more likely to replicate this pattern and develop fluent speech.

Type of dysfluent speech

As described in Chapter 1, there are different types of dysfluent speech. In preschool children it is especially important to observe the types of dysfluency they have. The reason for this is that some types of dysfluency are significant in predicting whether or not the stammer will persist into later life.

The key types of dysfluency to look out for are repetitions of:

- sounds (*r-r-r-red*)
- syllables (*wo-wo-wo-wolf*)
- monosyllabic words (*hood, hood, hood*).

These are more significant than repetitions of longer words (*grandma, grandma*) or phrases (*run away, run away*).

The number of times the repetitions occur is also important: the key number is three. If a child has repetitions with over three elements, e.g. *w-w-w-walk, ba-ba-ba-ba-basket* or *I, I, I, I*, this is considered more concerning than a child who says *w-walk, ba-basket* or *I, I*.

Other types of dysfluency are also significant with regard to the development of a persistent stammer:

- prolongation of sounds, such as *wwwwwood*
- extended silent periods where no sound is produced but the child appears to be trying to say something (*. . . chopping wood*)
- a disrupted breathing pattern, e.g. running out of or gasping for air when speaking, or taking multiple breaths before or during speech
- any behaviour which shows the child is struggling to speak, e.g. stamping his foot, tapping his fingers or closing his eyes.

Length of time the child has been stammering

If the child's speech has been dysfluent for over a year, this would be of concern and would indicate the need to refer to a specialist speech and language therapist.

Lack of change in the pattern of stammering

Another factor giving rise for concern is little variability or change in the child's speech over time, i.e. no periods where the stammering seems to diminish or disappear.

Child's response to the experience of stammering

Many children appear unaware of the level or severity of their dysfluency. Some may be aware but unconcerned by it, continuing to communicate in the same way and to the same extent. However, research has identified a group of children who appear generally more sensitive, less resilient and less able to control their emotional responses. This group is sensitive to any changes to their fluency and they react negatively to these differences.

Responses can include emotions such as anxiety, confusion, frustration and/or anger. These children may show changes in their behaviour which reflect these emotions. Some may try and change the way they speak in an attempt to exert control over the stammer. They may put on a funny voice or accent, or imitate a character from a television programme. They may talk more quietly or shout inappropriately. They may avoid saying certain words or stop speaking in situations where they anticipate difficulties.

Other children may exhibit a change in behaviours which are not directly associated with speaking, for example developing difficulties with sleeping, experiencing physical symptoms such as tummy ache or nausea, or withdrawing from play, interactions with other children and/or social situations.

This risk factor is very important and can impact on how the stammer develops over time and into adulthood. For this reason, let us look at it in more detail, using a useful analogy called the stammering iceberg.

Responses to stammering: the stammering iceberg

An American speech and language pathologist called Joseph Sheehan was the first person to talk about stammering using the metaphor of an iceberg. Sheehan used the iceberg to describe stammering because of its structure and appearance (see Figure 2.1): an observable or overt part above the waterline and a larger, hidden or covert part underneath the water.

- Overt or 'above the waterline' stammering – the overt part consists of what other people see and hear, such as the repetitions of sounds and syllables, the prolongation or stretching of sounds, silences or blocking, disrupted breathing and perhaps some struggling behaviours such as facial grimacing, jaw jerks, or arm and leg movements.
- Covert or 'hidden' stammering – the covert components of stammering are likely to be unobservable to an untrained listener and consist of the negative responses experienced by the child or young person to the stammer. These could include issues discussed in the previous section (e.g. sensitivity to stammering), avoidance behaviours (e.g. avoiding certain words or situations due to the fear of stammering) and negative thoughts (e.g. 'The class will laugh if I answer this question') or negative feelings (e.g. anger and frustration).

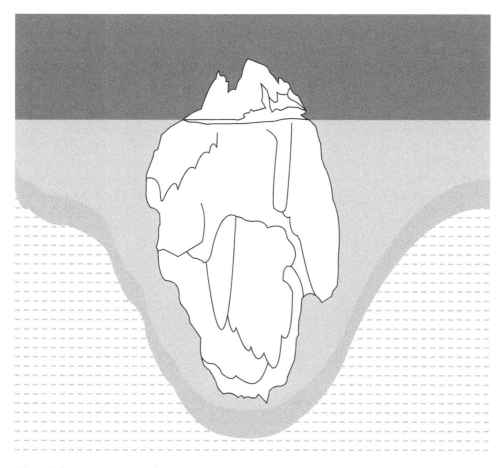

Figure 2.1

If we apply this to the development of stammering, it is clear that a young child would rarely have a covert component to his stammering at its onset, even if it seems very severe to an adult. Usually at this stage a child will have a completely 'overt' stammer. In other words, what we observe a young child doing is all of his stammer – 'what you see is what you get'. At this point he has not learnt to view or construe dysfluency as negative. He does not anticipate it or feel the need to change or avoid its occurrence. He may be aware of the dysfluency in the moment it happens but he does not carry this awareness into other situations. He does not think about the implications the disruption to his communication might have.

This lack of implication is a good place for a child to be and one which is likely to mean the child will develop positive coping strategies should the stammer persist. Any professionals working with a child at this stage will find it much easier to help him manage stammering speech because it is not complicated by unhelpful thoughts and feelings.

Changing awareness

As a child matures, his awareness of his abilities in relation to others becomes more acute. His awareness of stammering also changes and for some this can mean an increase in the level of concern. This may come about due to the influence of peers, comments made by other children or adults, or through the child's own sensitivity and emotional response to 'difference'.

Consequently, he comes to regard his stammering speech as unacceptable and feels the need to change his speech behaviour to avoid the disruptions when they occur. Sometimes he learns that stammering happens on a certain word, so he will avoid saying that word and substitute it for another, which may or may not be related in meaning. Or a pupil may realise that stammering happens at specific times, such as when talking in front of a group or asking the teacher a question in class, so then he chooses not to engage in the activity to avoid stammering. 'Show and tell' may become his worst activity rather that an opportunity to share something important or to impress his peers.

At this stage we see the development of features located below Sheehan's waterline: emotional responses to the dysfluency and avoidance behaviours. We may also notice changes in the pattern of stammering as the child tries to minimise its occurrence or how it appears. He could start to speak with more tension or at a faster rate in order to get it over and done with quickly. The volume of his speech may change as he experiments with speaking louder or more quietly to see the effect on his fluency. He may also try to control his fluency by changing his breathing pattern, for example by taking in double breath at the start of an utterance or saying what he needs to say on one breath.

While these small changes will not appear significant in isolation, they mark the start of a worrying change in the child. This change reflects the child's perception: 'the *way* I speak is more important than *what* I have to say'. Thus he is beginning to compromise his communication, and ultimately himself, for the sake of increased fluency.

Fear of stammering can mean a pupil chooses not to ask his teacher to clarify something he has not understood. He may fail to learn and this could impact upon his academic achievement in the long term. He may opt not to study academic subjects in which he has particular abilities because of the amount of speaking required, and then choose a career which does not fulfil his potential. He will ultimately not be the person he truly could be because of the compromises he has made to avoid stammering.

Why does stammering develop?

This section looks at one model that has been proposed to explain why stammering develops in a child. It is worth noting before we proceed that the current research points to a complex interaction of factors rather than one single explanation. However, the role of genetics and the neurological composition of a child's brain and its function are proving fertile areas of research. It could be that, in time, specific genetic components and/or differences in some neurological pathways will be identified as causal factors.

For clinicians and others working with children who stammer, this model helps us understand the often conflicting research evidence available.

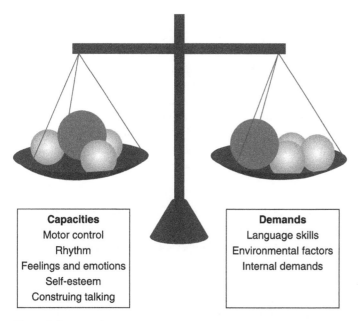

Capacities	**Demands**
Motor control	Language skills
Rhythm	Environmental factors
Feelings and emotions	Internal demands
Self-esteem	
Construing talking	

Figure 2.2

Demands and capacities model

The demands and capacities model was developed by Woody Starkweather in the late 1980s, with additional research in the following decade. In developing his model, Starkweather tried to make some sense of the often contradictory evidence on stammering in children.

This framework suggests that there are a number of factors that should be considered important in the development of stammering in children. No one factor is currently thought to be more significant than another. However, the combination of factors working together, in addition to the specific patterns of dysfluency the child has (see the previous section), may put a child at risk of developing persistent stammering.

This model may be better understood by imagining a set of scales or a balance (see Figure 2.2). This is a representation of the child's ability to be fluent. If the balance is overloaded on the demands side, the child experiences dysfluency. If it is overloaded on the alternative side, fluency results.

Starkweather explains in this model the various factors or weights which contribute to the tipping of the scales. On the left-hand side are the child's capacities which will develop as he matures, but will nonetheless play a part in the development of his ability to be fluent. Included here are the following capacities.

- **Motor control** – a child who has difficulty with large and fine muscle control is likely to struggle with the precise muscle movements required for production of sequences of sounds used in speaking.
- **Rhythm** – having a sense of rhythm helps a child predict the timing and melody of speech. This ability can help improve the fluency of a child's speech.

- **Feelings and emotions** – recent research has shown that a child who is more emotionally responsive and also struggles to contain his feelings, and one who appears to have a more sensitive temperament, is less able to manage the occurrence of disrupted communication.
- **Self-esteem** – an individual child with positive self-esteem and high self-confidence will be more able to manage any changes in his talking and will generally have more resilience to manage these difficulties.
- **Construing talking** – if a child can talk about his talking with others, including being able to articulate – even at a basic level – any issues he is experiencing, he will cope better. The problem may not disappear but, as with any issue, being able to talk it over with someone else seems to make it appear more manageable.

Aide was 3 and was at times dysfluent. He would repeat syllables several times and was acutely aware of what he was doing. A typical example occurred during one meal time when he asked for a drink. 'Mummy, I want ju-ju-ju-ju-ju-ju-ju- Oh! [frustrated] I can't say that. You say it, Mummy!'

He knew what he wanted to say, having identified the correct word, but could not complete it. He was monitoring his production and knew that it was going wrong. However, he was able to communicate his frustration to his mother and asked her to help him out. Together they discussed how words sometimes got stuck, especially when learning to speak in longer sentences and using lots of words, and that it was nothing to be concerned about.

Another preschool child, Miles was also dysfluent. In his case, these instances lasted several seconds and Miles managed them by changing his sentences, including changing the topic quite suddenly and on occasions stopping talking completely. He was not able to tell his parents what was happening and at times appeared unhappy and withdrawn. It seemed he was aware at some level of his difficulties but did not have the ability to be open about them. Instead he used strategies that had a negative effect on his self-esteem and made him unhappy.

It was suggested that his parents create opportunities for him to talk about what was happening in his speech and give him a better understanding. Once this was in place his behaviour improved and he started to comment on his dysfluencies, for example 'My words are a bit sticky today, Mummy.'

On the other side of the scales are a set of demands which can come from three main areas:

- demands on the child's language skills
- demands from the child's environment
- demands a child may place on himself, i.e. internal demands.

The following sections look briefly at each of these in turn.

Language demands

As language develops it creates its own set of demands for a child. First, a developing child gradually learns new words so the lexicon he has at his disposal increases over time. This means the child knows there is a 'right' word to convey his meaning and has to search for it in an increasingly growing 'pot' of options.

Second, he will move from speaking in short phrases to using much longer and more complex utterances that adhere to the grammatical rules of English, which he also must learn. In addition, his ability to accurately produce the sounds which make up a word improves with age. For example, *bid bad wut* (big bad wolf) is quite acceptable for a 2–3 year old but, by the time he reaches his fourth birthday, these sounds are usually produced more in line with adult articulation.

Finally, the growing child develops a knowledge of the social use of language. He learns when to talk, when not to interrupt others who are speaking, how to initiate conversations, how to ask questions and how to adjust the appropriateness of what he says according to whom he is speaking (i.e. what can be discussed with peers, and how to talk to adults who he knows and those he knows less well).

All of these factors will affect a child's ability to be fluent. As we will see later, we can help a child who is struggling to control his fluency by reducing the language demand he is experiencing. This may be by simplifying the response he is required to make, helping him organise his thoughts before speaking, reducing the complexity of the sentence structure or the articulation of the word, or perhaps by helping him understand the social context of his communication.

Environmental demands

A child does not exist in a vacuum: there are many factors that exist in his surroundings which can potentially create demand on his ability to communicate. Family, friends and school staff play an important part in these environmental issues. Let us consider some key factors.

- **Language levels used by others** – there is evidence that a child will try to emulate the level of language he hears others use with him. If this is slightly below or slightly above his normal usage, it will not create a problem. However, if the level is more difficult and outside his comfort zone, it will be hard for him to understand everything that is said to him and this creates a demand upon his communication.
- **Speech rate of others** – adults tend to speak more slowly to a younger child. Their rate increases naturally as a child gets older. Once again there is evidence that a child will try and match the rate of speech that he hears others use with him. His fluency will be compromised if the rate he is trying to use means he has less time to formulate, process and produce his own response, and does not enable him to sequence the muscle movements required to produce sounds.
- **Turn taking** – a child who is experiencing dysfluencies in his speech may have difficulty starting off speech. In some situations where there is quick-fire comment and response, or where someone is dominating an interaction, it may be difficult for the dysfluent child to have his turn: the window of opportunity is so small

that he is unable to process and coordinate his speech muscles to coincide with the opportunity to speak when it arises. In such a scenario, children can react in different ways; one child may withdraw and feel unable to risk loss of fluency in such a competitive environment, while another may appear rude as his response is mistimed and he talks over others.

- **Urgency** – both speech rate and rapid turn taking can affect a child's perception of the urgency of a communication situation. In addition, he can be aware of a general sense of 'hurriedness' where activities are carried out in a rushed way or when a child is encouraged to increase the pace of his behavior, e.g. 'You only have five minutes to finish this so please hurry up.' A child needs to understand time constraints around certain actions, but it is important he also has sufficient time to process and organise his thoughts and behaviours. This will allow him to produce the best result he can. When this is compromised it will create an added demand on his fluency.

- **Demand speech** – adults demand speech of a child in all sorts of ways:
    - o social niceties or what some may call politeness (e.g. 'say thank you' or 'say please')
    - o corrections to expressive speech (e.g. '"get" not "gotten"', 'don't say it in that singsong voice, speak up')
    - o situations in which information is required or content is specified (e.g. 'what happened yesterday?', 'where is your homework?')
    - o responses that must be directed at a specific person (e.g. 'tell the teacher about . . .').

On occasions, several of these demands may occur simultaneously, for example: 'Here is Mr Lyndsey, the head teacher. Talk to him and tell him about your class trip yesterday to the zoo.') Here the child's communication choices have been removed: he is required to speak in that moment, to a certain person and about a specific topic. These demands change a child from a spontaneous speaker to a performer and may outweigh a child's ability or desire to talk.

- **Specific events** – a child can become excited or stressed about new or out-of-the-ordinary activities that may be obvious to adults, but can be a context in which a child experiences a demand on his fluency. Some events create positive emotion, such as a special outing or a new visitor. Some increase anxiety and tension, such as moving house, beginning school, the birth of a new sibling, or family issues including separation and divorce. For a child whose fluency is at risk, we should be alert to the effect these events can have on his speech.

- **Reactions to dysfluent speech** – the child may or may not be aware of the disruption in his speech. However, it is likely that the adults around him – his family members and school staff – will be. When and how these adults react to the fluency and dysfluencies will have an influence on the child. He may be puzzled about comments on dysfluency and praise for fluent speech, and not understand why adults make comments or seem concerned. Alternatively, others' reactions may contribute to a change in his level of awareness and increase his sensitivity to the stammer. If the child is worried or fearful of others' reactions to his speech, this will create a desire to manage his level of fluency and to try to reduce the frequency of overt stammering.

Internal demands

Research has shown a positive link between children with certain traits and the risk of persistent stammering. It is recommended that adults working with children who show dysfluencies at a young age are alert to a number of characteristics which can be significant:

- perfectionism or poor tolerance of errors in self and others
- reluctant risk taking
- high expectations of self without the necessary aptitude, practice or maturity
- concern about the implications of getting things wrong
- frustration with learning a new task or skill.

It is easy to see how these characteristics may contribute to anxiety in certain circumstances. If a child is experiencing speech disruptions then the following factors may also apply:

- worrying about the consequences
- being frustrated that speech is not fluent
- not risking speaking if he thinks he is going to stammer
- expecting to be dysfluent in situations where there is high communicative demand (e.g. speaking in front of a group or speaking when he is not sure about the content of his utterance).

Key points to remember

- Stammering usually starts between the ages of 2 and 5, with a mean age of around 3½ years.
- The dysfluencies may be severe at first but this is not significant in terms of whether/how it will later develop.
- Children, especially boys, can take a while to spontaneously recover.
- There are a number of identifiable risk factors for persistent stammering:

  o   gender
  o   genetics
  o   types of dysfluent episodes
  o   length of time a child is dysfluent
  o   lack of change in the pattern of dysfluencies
  o   the child's response to the dysfluencies.

- Stammering begins with all its characteristics visible 'above the waterline'.
- Over time, some features such as emotional and psychological reactions to stammering can become hidden. This makes stammering more difficult to manage.
- A useful model for understanding stammering and how it may present in a child is the demands and capacities model.

3   Problems with fluency in preschool children

Zain started nursery just before his third birthday. He appeared to be a bright child and his language skills, particularly his vocabulary, were thought to be in advance of his age.

After a few weeks, staff noticed a sudden onset of dysfluent speech when he was asking permission to do something and asking questions generally. This could last for several seconds and was especially apparent in the morning session at nursery. Zain seemed to be aware of his difficulties and had recently begun to change words and give up his attempts to speak when the dysfluencies occurred.

Some staff reported that he would sometimes stop and start saying 'doobie, doobie' instead of finishing his sentence. His general behaviour was also different; he changed from being outgoing and demonstrative to being quite quiet and withdrawn.

Introduction

It is important to see disruptions in a child's level of fluency in the context of his environment, be it home, school or another setting. In this chapter we explore the nature of a preschool class and identify some of the factors that can contribute to the child's fluency. Some of these factors may work positively, while others will disrupt the child's ability to control his speech. Many of the issues will be familiar to teachers as general demands that are placed on pupils, but others may be surprising in the context of helping a child maintain fluent speech.

This chapter will explain in detail how a teacher might manage the occurrence of dysfluency in a pupil at this early stage of education. A four-step programme is described with additional practical ways of changing the classroom environment to help the child keep better control of his talking.

Starting school

Starting school for the first time is a daunting prospect for any child. There are many challenges that he will face and will have to learn to manage in this new phase of his life.

In Chapter 2 the idea of a balance of demands and capacities was discussed, explaining the variability in dysfluencies in different children and also within the same child. It is useful to apply this same model to the experience of starting school, and to consider what demands might affect the pupil and what effect they could have on his speech.

Demands which might arise from starting school

Separation anxiety

Starting school may be a child's first experience of separation anxiety. It can be the first time he has been left for any length of time by a parent or carer who has been his companion and source of security since birth. This can be a cause of great concern and require huge adjustment.

Many nurseries manage this very well, for example with staff from the nursery meeting the pupil in his own home before he starts. There may well be additional 'getting to know you' visits to the nursery and a gradual build-up to the individual attending a full nursery session.

Change of environment

In coming to nursery he will have to learn what goes where, how and where to find different things, and the venue within the nursery for different activities. He will need to develop a sense of the geography of the classroom and the wider setting of the nursery. He will come to place the nursery in relation to his home or, at very least, its place in relation to other classrooms if it is located within a primary school.

Change in social interaction

The child's social interaction will no longer be just with a parent or carer but he will have to interact with many different adults. In doing this he will need to learn about sharing adults' time and attention, and he will develop an understanding of the different roles that adults play (e.g. those involved in education and working in a classroom, and others perhaps in the office or kitchen).

His circle of friends suddenly becomes wider. He may have previously attended mums and tots, music, massage and/or storytelling groups, but now he will be mixing with lots of children of his own age and within one small physical space. Consequently, he will have to learn more about negotiation, sharing toys and activities, and how to play, interact and communicate with small and large groups of children.

As part of this process, he may try out a variety of roles: being the leader, remaining outside the main group, being funny, being physical and boisterous. He may also experiment with different styles of communication: directing play and telling other children what to do, saying silly things, being inquisitive and/or choosing not to speak at certain times.

Behaviour

The child will be required to manage his own behaviour in a way he has not been asked to previously. This will involve following routines and regulating his behaviour in different settings, e.g. on the carpet, during circle time, in front of the whiteboard.

Learning

He will also be asked to engage in learning new skills, and his progress in acquiring these skills will be closely monitored by others. This may suggest to a pupil that learning certain pieces of information is important and he may feel judged or perhaps engage in competition with others around certain activities.

Impact of nursery

Finally, many parents report that their child is very tired at the end of his nursery session. Teachers will be aware of this and often recommend to parents that the child may need more sleep, be less tolerant of things, and be more easily upset or angered as his tolerance is compromised by fatigue. This tiredness can be reflected in his speech and language, too; sometimes a child is more reluctant to communicate and needs more quiet time. Other children appear to increase their rate of speech and be unable to regulate their turn taking, volume and output generally.

Looking out for dysfluency in preschool children

In the majority of cases stammering starts during the preschool years, around the age of 3½ years. It is therefore likely that a preschool teacher or other school professional may notice the first signs of dysfluency in a child. It is extremely important that the signs of persistent stammering are spotted early and that examples of normal non-fluency are managed appropriately. Early years professionals are in the ideal situation to play this role.

Monitoring a preschool child's fluency

To facilitate appropriate monitoring in preschool settings, Figure 3.1 presents the signs and potential pathway of normal dysfluency to persistent stammering which a child might follow.

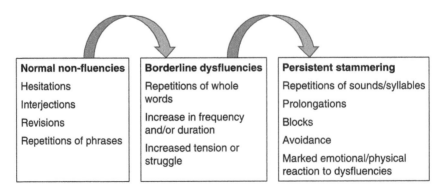

Normal non-fluencies	Borderline dysfluencies	Persistent stammering
Hesitations	Repetitions of whole words	Repetitions of sounds/syllables
Interjections		Prolongations
Revisions	Increase in frequency and/or duration	Blocks
Repetitions of phrases		Avoidance
	Increased tension or struggle	Marked emotional/physical reaction to dysfluencies

Figure 3.1

In the early years of development, a child can show a number of different types of dysfluencies in his speech. To the uninitiated these may all seem like disruptions in his talking, which of course they are. However, in terms of the development of stammering, some are more significant than others. These differences in speech in a child can occur very close together in time. Adults may not be aware of the subtle changes that have taken place and can perceive that the final stage (persistent stammering) is the start of the child's difficulties.

Normal non-fluencies and language

Some dysfluencies reflect the child's early processing of language: the search for the 'right' word, sorting out the order of the words in a sentence, working out how to explain something which is quite lengthy or complex, etc. These dysfluencies are normal and relate to what, in the demands and capacities model outlined in the previous chapter, we have called the child's language capacity.

Normal non-fluencies and motor skills

Another child may have difficulties articulating the sequence of sounds that form a word. This may be due to the nature of the sounds involved – even as adults, we find some words more difficult to say than others.

Alternatively, it may be due to the motor requirements of the utterance, i.e. the proximity or lack of proximity of the tongue or lip placement which is required to say the sounds in a sequence. (This is the basis on which 'tongue twisters' operate; for example, 'red lorry, yellow lorry' is difficult to say because the sounds are produced in locations which are quite far apart in the mouth. In contrast, 'she sells sea shells on the sea shore' works as a tongue twister because the sounds involved are produced close together in the mouth.)

A child's ability to move his articulators (tongue, lips, palate and jaw) increases with age. As he grows and matures he will become more adept at moving them at speed and his brain will be able to send the nerve impulses required much more quickly. The difficulties associated with an immature nervous and motor system relate to what we have called the child's motor capacity and, to a lesser extent, his rhythmical skills.

Both of these sorts of issues are likely to give rise to the features known as normal non-fluencies. As described in Chapter 1, the features of normal non-fluencies would generally be:

- repetitions of phrases and some words
- revisions (i.e. when the child starts by saying one thing then corrects or interrupts himself to say something else), for example 'I want the key cars . . . car keys'
- *errs* and *umms* that are also heard in adult speech
- some silent pauses or time for thinking.

Significant changes in speech

Researchers have identified several changes in dysfluencies which indicate a move from normal developmental dysfluency to stammering. These are summarised as follows.

CHANGES IN *TYPE*

- The dysfluencies are characterised by repetitions of smaller portions of words: syllables (*I like tru-tru-tru-trucks*) and/or sounds (*C-c-c-cars aren't as fast*).
- There is more struggle and tension in the moment of the dysfluency, resulting in the occurrence of prolongations of some sounds (*sssssuper fast*) and blocking when attempting to say a sound, particularly at the start of an utterance (*. . . I want that tractor*).

CHANGES IN *SEVERITY*

- The disruptions in speech are more frequent.
- The disruptions are longer in duration.

CHANGES IN *TIMING* OF WHEN THE DYSFLUENCIES OCCUR

- The dysfluencies occur with more predictability in certain situations, on specific words, and/or with particular people.
- Their occurrence is less variable and the times when they are not present becomes less.

Anyone working with preschool children should be aware of these significant changes in the pattern of dysfluency and look out for them. However, one of the striking features of early dysfluency in children is the way it comes and goes. Parents report that a child can have periods of marked disruption to his speech followed by weeks of fluent speech. Even within a day, a child may experience significant variability in his speech. This can be frustrating for everyone. Parents or carers and family members are unsure whether or not to be concerned. They often book appointments for the child to be seen by a family doctor or speech and language therapist, and then feel embarrassed at the child's level of fluency while in the appointment or assessment session.

One important point to note about this variability is that generally if the dysfluency becomes linked to specific places, people and/or aspects of language, and is therefore less variable, our level of concern should increase.

A final point of significance is the child's awareness and his own level of concern. Sometimes a child can have marked disruptions in his speech, long repetitions or frequent revisions, and he appears unaware and unconcerned. The adults around him may be more acutely aware of the dysfluencies and feel this is a problem that needs addressing. They may want to manage the problem because of their own level of concern or embarrassment, or because others in the family or social circle have mentioned it and are finding it hard to cope with.

The key point here is that a preschool pupil does not need to have his attention drawn to disruptions in his speech. Highlighting the occurrence of dysfluencies to a child who has little awareness can result in him trying to modify his speech, which makes the dysfluencies worse. He may try to change the way he speaks and in doing so his speech takes on more significant patterns of dysfluency, which involve struggle and/or increased tension. A more productive way of managing disruptions is through subtle changes to the pupil's environment, for example making the language level easier or modelling an easier production for him in response. For example:

Child:	*C-c-c-can I go – can I go out to Aaaaaaa* [stops, takes a breath] *Aaaaaadam's house?*
Parent/adult:	*To Adam's* [said with a soft start on the A] *house? Yes, let's ring his Mum and find out when is a good time.*

There will be more about how to manage persistent stammering later on.

Managing the risk of persistent stammering in preschool settings

There are four-steps that can be used to change the classroom environment to help the child keep better control of his talking.

Step 1: Monitor and observe

Dysfluent speech

The first step in developing a plan to help a preschool child who dysfluent is to explore the nature of the dysfluencies. You need to have information on the following:

- **The what** – what do the disruptions sound like, i.e. repetitions of sounds, syllables or phrases, prolongations of sounds, blocks? Is breathing affected? Does he appear tense and struggle to speak?
- **The how** – as well as the type of dysfluencies observed, it is also useful to notice the frequency of the dysfluencies. This gives an indication of how much variability occurs. Monitoring this over time will identify periods of improvement or deterioration in the pupil's level of fluency.
- **The where** – in what situations and with whom do the dysfluencies occur?
- **The when** – when do the disruptions happen, e.g. when the pupil is asking a question or when he is explaining something? In the morning session or at the end of the day?

It is suggested that these observations be carried out during the course of nursery attendance and/or over a number of days or weeks. Sometimes different people have different sensitivities and perceptions of dysfluencies so it is helpful to allocate the same member of staff to this task throughout the observation. This improves the reliability and consistency of the observations, especially when carried out over a longer period of time.

A checklist is provided to help staff structure their observations and record the significant details covered in this section.

Dysfluencies: An observational checklist for preschool staff		
Examples of normal non-fluencies	✓ /✗	*When/where*
Hesitations (*I, er, um* [pause] *want to paint a picture*) Interjections (*You know, I want to paint a picture*) Revisions (*I want, James says, can I paint a picture?*) Repetitions of phrases (*I want, I want, I want to paint*)		

(Continued)

(Continued)

Examples of borderline dysfluencies	✓/✗	When/where
Repetitions of whole words (*I, I, I want to paint*) Increase in frequency and/or duration Increased tension or struggle (e.g. pushing sound out)		

Risk of persistent stammering	✓/✗	When/where
Repetitions of sounds, syllables (*I w-w-want to p-p-paint*) Prolongations (*Mmmmiss, I want to paint*) Blocks ([silence] *I want to paint*) Breathing disruptions before or during speaking, e.g. multiple intakes of air, running out of air ([in breath ×2] *I want to paint*) Marked physical reaction, e.g. facial tension, body movements Avoidance of saying certain sounds, words and/or avoiding speaking (*I want to . . . James has got his apron on*) Marked emotional reaction, e.g. gives up speaking, becomes upset/angry		

The communication context

First, look at the communication dynamics in the classroom by considering the following.

- **Level of language used** – including the complexity of words and sentence structures, and the use of difficult vocabulary or words outside the pupil's expected level of understanding.
- **Number and type of questions used** – is the pupil asked multiple questions at one time? Is he given the chance to answer single questions before being presented with additional ones? Are direct or open-ended questions used?
- **Turn taking and the dynamics in group and large classroom activities** – does the pupil have plenty of time to speak? Do children vie for communication turns? Do children wait for each other to speak and are they able to complete their sentences?
- **Pace of conversation** – do adults in the classroom create enough opportunity for a pupil to make a comment or answer a question? This would be especially important for a child who has slower language processing and/or immature motor programming of speech.
- **Initiating speech** – is it easy for the pupil to ask an adult a direct question in the classroom?
- **Interruptions** – when other individuals are talking, how are interruptions by a pupil managed?
- **Use of demand speech** – does the teaching style involve asking a pupil questions with a specific answer and in a context where there is a short response time?

A checklist is provided to help staff structure their observations and record these significant details.

Communication context: An observational checklist for preschool staff

Level of language used	✓/✗	When/where
Are complex words and sentence structures in use? Is there use of difficult vocabulary or words outside the pupil's expected level of understanding?		
Number and type of questions used	✓/✗	When/where
Is the pupil asked multiple questions at one time? Is he given the chance to answer single questions before being presented with additional ones? Are direct or open-ended questions used?		
Turn taking and the dynamics in group and large classroom activities	✓/✗	When/where
Does the pupil have plenty of time to speak? Do children vie for communication turns? Do children wait for each other to speak? Do children complete the sentences of others?		
Pace of conversation	✓/✗	When/where
Do adults create enough opportunity for the pupil to make a comment or answer a question?		
Initiating speech	✓/✗	When/where
Is it easy for the pupil to ask an adult a direct question?		
Interruptions	✓/✗	When/where
Are interruptions by a pupil appropriately managed?		
Use of demand speech	✓/✗	When/where
Is the pupil asked questions with a specific answer? Is there a short response time?		

Second, examine your own speaking style. As previously discussed, there is an interaction between the adult's and the pupil's use of language and delivery of speech, especially with regard to speech rate. These features can impact on the level of fluency the child has in a situation. Consequently, they need to be explored in relation to teachers' and assistants' speaking, particularly when staff are addressing the dysfluent pupil individually.

In addition to those features considered when looking at the communication dynamics listed above, there are features that are pertinent to a one-to-one situation with a child:

- Non-verbal behaviour – specifically a teacher's non-verbal reactions when the pupil is dysfluent and her skill at keeping good eye contact with him when he is talking

- Speech rate
- Use of pauses at the beginning of speech – especially after being asked a question, and during longer utterances, e.g. when explaining something to the pupil.

If there are support systems in place within the preschool environment for staff to provide feedback to each other, then these factors could be included in any review exercise.

Finally, it is useful to consider how a teacher feels when she hears a pupil stammer. There can be difficulties in listening to stammering. Sometimes the listener recalls times when she, or someone close to her, was dysfluent and experienced anxiety as a result. A listener may have an intolerance of disrupted communication and/or slower speech rate in others and finds herself feeling irritated. In other circumstances waiting for a pupil to finish off a sentence in a particular situation is difficult. Examples might be when other children are competing for attention, when there is a time constraint built in to the situation (e.g. 'we have to go to the hall now') or where the teacher has other priorities, such as preventing a pupil from being hurt.

It is important to accept individual responses to the pupil's dysfluency, remembering that we all have our own tolerance levels for a variety of speech differences. However, if our response is one that compounds the problem, we should think about other ways of managing it. Remember the child at this stage is rarely aware of doing anything different with his talking, so it is vital that listeners do not give him the message that his speech is in some way unacceptable and needs to be changed: this can lead to the child making modifications that compromise his communication and make it more difficult to resolve in the long term.

Exploration of a teacher's speaking style and demonstrating acceptance of a pupil's dysfluency are areas where a specialist speech and language therapist would be able to help.

Step 2: Find out what the pupil thinks about talking

The next step is to create a situation in which the child can talk about talking in general and his speech in particular. The key aspect of this conversation is to create a sense of informality for the pupil and a spirit of openness. It is important that the individual is enabled to share his feelings as appropriate and does not feel judged or criticised in any way.

This could be achieved in a small group, perhaps in a free play situation, when the topic of talking can be broached. The group may be asked to discuss such topics as how they learnt to talk, whether they have watched how babies learn to talk, whether they find talking difficult and if so in which situations it is difficult and in which situations it is easy. To promote the sharing of experience, an adult can give an example of when she finds talking difficult and situations when it is easy (e.g. 'Some words are harder for me to say. I always find the word "statistics" hard to say. I have to give myself time to think about the word before saying it.') This general conversation may suit some pupils if the group constitutes a safe environment. Other preschoolers may prefer a one-to-one conversation with an adult around the same topic.

Another way of finding out the pupil's perspective is to discuss it in the moment of dysfluency. When a teacher notices the child struggling on a word and is fairly sure the child has noticed too, she can make a single comment such as: 'Oh, that was a hard word for you to say. Does that happen a lot? Why do you think it happens? What do you normally do when you have a hard word to say?' The number of follow-up questions will of course depend on the pupil's initial response to the question, including their non-verbal behaviours. If he says he has not noticed or it doesn't happen, then the topic should not be pursued. However, if the child comments on its frequency and aspects of severity, this provides an opportunity to support and/ or reassure him.

Step 3: Talk to the parents

Having established the nature of the problem in the preschool, it is now time to try and find out how the context is contributing to its occurrence. We know that dysfluency in early years is very variable and in some cases may be situation specific. A preschool pupil often experiences disruptions to his speech when managing difficult situations, especially those that he is experiencing for the first time. It is, therefore, important to have a conversation as soon as possible with a parent or carer to see if the dysfluency is also apparent at home or in other family situations.

A conversation in which the nature and frequency of dysfluency in nursery is discussed as the sole topic may give rise to anxiety in parents, especially if they had not noticed it themselves. Rather than this be the main focus of a conversation, it would be more helpful to raise the issue generally, such as when their child's overall progress in preschool is discussed, e.g. at a parents' evening with a general introduction to the topic such as: 'How do you think Zac's speech is coming along?' As the conversation develops, aspects of the observational checklist could be shared in ways which downplay the pupil's difficulty, for example: 'We have done some detailed observations of him in nursery over the last two weeks and his speech bumps only happen a couple of times a day. We have noticed them when he talks with Rachel but never when he is playing cars with Thomas.'

Parents should be encouraged to talk about times when they have noticed any difficulties, when others have commented on the child's speech, and occasions when there were no problems. (It can be reassuring for parents to know that variability is not linked to persistence but to recovery.) In circumstances in which the parents are not aware of any difficulty or have not been monitoring the child's speech directly at home, it can be useful to suspend the discussion until they have had an opportunity to carry out observations themselves.

It is *not* recommended that teachers give them the classroom checklist for use at home: this can create unnecessary anxiety and may lead to confusion over differences between normal non-fluencies and the signs of persistent stammering. A better option is for the parents to be directed to more general observation of their child's speech in specific contexts such as:

* relaxed times
* pressurised times (e.g. getting ready for school)
* times when he is tired
* interacting with other family members/siblings and when speaking to people he knows less well.

If the speech difficulty seems to be linked to preschool attendance and does not seem to be present in other situations, this would indicate the need for a specific school management plan. If its occurrence is more general and the more significant types of dysfluency are present at home in addition to at school, then the need for a referral to a specialist speech and language therapist should be discussed with the parents.

Step 4: Put a plan in place

Using the principles of the demands and capacities model discussed in Chapter 2, the aims of producing a plan are to develop the pupil's capacities and reduce the demands being made on him in the preschool setting.

Developing capacities

1. Maximise fluency – when a pupil is having a day when his speech is naturally more fluent, this would be an ideal time to ask him to speak more in a variety of situations. A child is naturally more fluent singing, talking to animals, and when speaking in unison or alongside another person or child. These situations can be used to good effect when the child needs to experience more fluency. It is important not to overly praise a pupil for his fluency as this can lead him to attend to his level of fluency.

> Aran was having a particularly bumpy time with his speech. However, the nursery teacher gave him responsibility that day to feed the class guinea pigs. She gave him instructions about what to do which included telling him to tell the guinea pigs a story, The Three Little Pigs. Aran knew the story well so it was not difficult for him to formulate the language required. Talking to the animals gave him the opportunity to have a fluent period of speech which helped his confidence for that session in nursery.

2. Increase the time the child has to process and produce language – adults working with the pupil should be directed to pause before answering his questions, use a slower speaking rate, and use more pauses in their speech when speaking with him.
3. Develop his fine and gross motor skills.
4. Develop his rhythmical skills.
5. Develop self-esteem and confidence – keep eye contact and do not speak for him when he is dysfluent. Use praise, not only for good communication but for good behaviour as appropriate. Develop his level of responsibility by giving him small tasks to do or roles to play in the class.
6. Provide emotional support – the child may need help to manage his feelings when experiencing dysfluency. He may get frustrated or angry or feel upset without necessarily understanding why. Teachers can help by validating and acknowledging the pupil's feelings, providing reassurance and/or distraction at the right time.

7. Managing perfectionism and/or sensitivity to dysfluency in the pupil and others working with him – some individuals with dysfluent speech also have poor tolerance of errors. A pupil like this who experiences imperfections in his speech can become frustrated and angry. It may be important in these cases to teach an acceptance of errors and help the child appreciate the 'journey of learning'.

> *Joel hated drawing as he could never perform to the level of skill he demanded of himself. Consequently he would give up as soon as his attempts were less than perfect. Helping him tolerate mistakes in his drawing was useful and enabled him to be more tolerant of the bumps in his speech when they happened.*

8. Help the pupil to feel the same as his peer group – work on including him in situations that require speaking out. Give him the opportunity to talk if he wishes to and, if it proves to be difficult for him, make sure the language level he uses is at a lower level and he has the appropriate level of support to speak.
9. Open up dialogue – provide the pupil with opportunities to talk about talking.

Reducing demands

1. A teacher in a one-to-one conversation with the dysfluent pupil should use a somewhat simpler language level and thereby enable him to simplify his own language.
2. Change and/or modify questioning technique – a teacher can use questions to help reduce the language demand in a conversation. She can help him to structure his responses by using questions, making his sentences shorter and less complex.
   Example 1: Teacher: 'Tell me about your drawing.'
   This is a question that demands the pupil does a lot of work to organise and structure his response.
   Example 2: Teacher: 'Tell me about your drawing. I am particularly interested in the colour. Why did you use blue? [child responds] Ah, I see. Now tell me about the house. Is that the same as the house you live in?'
   The pupil is directed to address specific aspects of his drawing, rather than explaining it to her as a whole. In addition, the teacher is encouraging the child to use simpler language as her questions are specific.
3. Increase the window of opportunity for the pupil's responses – allow him time to respond and create a listening environment where he will not fear interruptions.
4. Work on classroom dynamics – encourage good turn taking, including sharing turns, and minimise interruptions from other children. Create opportunities for the child to engage with a trusted peer/assistant and to be in a non-competitive or quiet speaking environment without distractions. This is especially important when his level of fluency is reduced.
5. Reactions to non-fluency – ensure other pupils respond appropriately when the child is dysfluent. Look out for mimics, although this happens less often in preschool years as young children do not appear to notice dysfluencies in their peers. The

teacher should also monitor her own non-verbal behaviour when the child is dysfluent.

It is important that teachers do not feel the need to teach preschool pupils to talk differently. At this early stage the objective is to watch and identify both the features in the environment that can be modified and the competencies of the child that can be enhanced in order to better manage the dysfluency.

If the school staff believe that the pupil is consistently showing signs of persistent stammering, they should contact a specialist speech and language therapist for additional help and advice.

Key points to remember

- The pupil has a set of capacities that can be enhanced to help him manage early signs of dysfluency.
- There are demands in the environment that affect a pupil's fluency.
- There are differences between normal non-fluency, which is a developmental stage in children, and persistent stammering.
- Changes in the type, severity and timing of normal non-fluency can suggest a move to the risk of persistent stammering.
- The specific signs of persistent stammering in preschool pupils need to be monitored closely over time.
- Referral to a specialist speech and language therapist is recommended when the signs of persistent stammering appear.
- Open up dialogue with the pupil about talking in general and, if appropriate, about how he feels about his talking.
- The child's awareness and level of concern is significant at this stage. It is important not to draw a pupil's attention to his dysfluency but to acknowledge any emotional response he has when he has speech difficulties.
- Any management plan for the pupil should consist of an observation phase, engaging the parents, managing the environmental demands, developing the child's capacities, and enlisting the help of a specialist speech and language therapist
- Teaching the pupil to talk differently is *not* appropriate at this stage: 'Fluency is not a goal for the teacher' (British Stammering Association advice).

Dos and don'ts for the preschool stage of dysfluency

Things to do	*Things to avoid*
Observe occurrences of dysfluency	Don't try and change a pupil's speaking pattern
Notice type of dysfluency	Don't criticise dysfluent speech
Notice when dysfluency occurs	Don't praise fluent speech
Notice changes in severity	Don't interrupt a pupil's speaking turn
Ascertain the level of the pupil's awareness	Don't tell him/her to alter his speech

Reduce language demand when a pupil is dysfluent, i.e. demand less complex language	Don't demand responses with complex language
Reduce direct questions	Don't use direct questions
Allow a pupil to choose to respond	Don't single a pupil out to make a verbal response
Manage negative responses from peer group to stammering	Don't allow ridicule or mimicking of the pupil's stammer
Keep eye contact with the pupil when he is speaking	Don't look away when he stammers
Provide support and reassurance	Don't talk for the pupil
Talk to parents about their child's speech, generally and specifically related to stammering	Don't fill in stammered words (unless this has been negotiated with the pupil beforehand)
Refer to a specialist speech and language therapist	
Give the pupil time to talk	Don't rush the pupil's speaking turn
Include the pupil in speaking opportunities	Don't assume he will not wish to take part in verbal activities or performance
Develop his self-confidence, perhaps by giving him responsibility within class	
Use a slower speech rate when talking to the pupil	
Ask colleagues to review your communication style	

4   Problems with fluency
in primary school pupils

> Sam is 8 and goes to the primary school in his village. He has been dysfluent since he was in nursery but it never seemed to be an issue for him. Recently, his speaking difficulties have been having more of an impact, especially on his moods. He came home from school one day and was very quiet. When asked if anything was bothering him, he became angry and uncharacteristically threw one of his toys on the floor.
>
>   Later, at bedtime, he told his mother that some older children had laughed at his talking and had asked him why he 't-t-talked' like that. Sam said he didn't know what to do and was upset. In subsequent days Sam was reluctant to go to school and had bouts of 'tummy ache' at breakfast time.

Introduction

As he progresses through his school, a primary school pupil will experience significant social development. These developments often create demands on his communication skills, especially in the context of the classroom. In this chapter the various demands will be outlined, alongside the changes that may be occurring in how the child's speech fluency looks and sounds from the outside and feels for the child on the inside.

In the primary school years a child experiences significant changes in his social development. These changes affect what is demanded of his communication competence. The key features of social development in these years are:

- A decrease in dependence on parents and/or carers who featured strongly in the preschool years. As the number and type of adults with whom a pupil relates extends in these years, the amount of influence any one particular individual exerts diminishes. Parents are no longer the sole 'wisdom' in the child's world. Rather, the child has a growing sense of knowledge spread across a number of resources or groups of individuals. Thus parents 'know stuff' about meals, transport etc. but teachers 'know stuff' about the Romans, what will happen in class etc.
- The development of the importance of the peer group. While parents' influence diminishes, that of the peer group increases. The child may appear less willing to accept advice from adults, preferring to follow peers instead. The number and range

of friends becomes greater and the child learns to change and adapt to different friendship groups. Problems can occur as groups and roles within groups change (of which more later in this chapter).

- The pupil will face peer pressure and experience criticism and judgement from the group, along with validation and reward. The group can contribute to the pupil's understanding of social acceptability and an awareness of himself in a social context. However, the power of the group can negatively impact on his self-esteem if he learns from group members that he is inferior in some way. In addition, he may have to make choices that at times set him apart from group members or which enable him to conform to a group norm on other occasions.
- A pupil of this age often experiences a number of complex emotions, many of which will be familiar to adults. However, he does not always have the capacity to understand his feelings, nor give voice to his experiences. This can mean some emotions are difficult for him to manage and he may react with behaviours that are out of character.
- A primary school pupil needs help in developing an objective stance when faced with a problem. His natural tendency will be to react from his perspective and fail to see opposing views or alternatives. He will require practice to develop different perspectives and the objectivity required to solve problems appropriately.

Stammering and the primary school pupil

A primary school pupil will still be experiencing developmental changes in his language. His ability to understand and process verbal information develops rapidly at this age, as does his competency in producing complex and lengthy sentence structures and the adult forms of English. In most children these developmental milestones progress without problem but for some, especially boys, they take a little more time.

Any delays or difficulties in speech and language in primary school pupils can occur in parallel to a stammer which, at this point, will have been around for some time. The child may well have been stammering on and off for years. It is probable that there have been changes both in the presentation of his stammer and his response to it.

Changes in the stammer

Repetitions

As shown in Chapter 3 (Figure 3.1), the development of the stammer involves increasing fragmentation of the units of speech. Consequently, a primary school pupil is more likely to repeat words or parts of words such as syllables.

Occurrence

The occurrences or frequency of the speech disruptions often increase. The time taken by each dysfluency also extends at this age, moving from brief moments of disruption to more-lengthy events. The dysfluencies can become more consistent and begin to be linked to certain situations, such as the register or speaking in front of the class.

Increased tension or struggle

As the pupil attempts to control or extricate himself from the stammering, he often uses more force or effort. His speech muscles become tense and as a result his breathing is disrupted, and articulation is harder and pushed out. In more severe instances there may be times when his whole speaking system is locked by tension.

Changes in the pupil's response to his stammer

Awareness

In preschool years, the dysfluency is often fleeting and the child may or may not have some sense of difficulty in the moment. However, with increasing occurrences and possible extended dysfluencies, the primary school pupil can become more aware of his speech disruptions. For some children the awareness does not lead to any further changes: he knows that his speech sometimes is 'bumpy' but, in the same way as a sneeze, it passes and has no great impact on how he communicates.

> When discussing getting 'stuck' on words, Rhiannon agreed that it did sometimes happen to her. A follow-up question attempted to ascertain what strategies she used. She said: 'I just go and ask my mum what the word says.' Her response indicated that getting stuck was something she associated with reading and not her spontaneous speech, despite the fact that listeners would hear dysfluencies in both situations.

For other pupils the knowledge that speech can be problematic results in other physical, cognitive and emotional changes.

PHYSICAL RESPONSES

In essence, a stammer is experienced by a child as speaking 'out of control'. In attempting to exert control on this event, the child tenses his speech muscles, including his diaphragm, laryngeal muscles, tongue and/or lips. (This is in fact the opposite of what is required, as relaxation would help him better control his stammer. However, this goes against the natural instinct of the child at this age and is hard to achieve.) The increased tension will certainly worsen the stammer.

A listener may notice instances, especially at the beginning of an utterance, where the child's speaking is frozen or locked. The pupil can get stuck on a particular sound, stretch its production and appear unable to move on to the next sound in the word, e.g. *wwwwwhere*. On other occasions, he will be unable to initiate any sound at all and is said to be 'blocking'.

Both of these examples signify a move to a more persistent form of stammering. This can be upsetting for the pupil and may well be noticed by his peers and/or adults. Undoubtedly he will wish to minimise their occurrence and may try to impose control through more of the 'forcing' strategy. Alternatively, a child will shut down his talking altogether and choose not to say his target word or give up speaking completely.

COGNITIVE RESPONSES

A primary school pupil is engaged in learning about himself in different situations. The occurrence of increasing speech difficulties for a child who has a particular temperament can mean he thinks negatively about himself. Specifically, an individual who is less resilient, more sensitive and less tolerant of his mistakes will begin to think that he is unable to talk properly in those situations where he has noticed stammering or when it has been brought to his attention. He will begin to engage in negative self-talk such as 'I can't do this', 'Ali is better at talking than me' or 'I'm not going to put my hand up to answer that question (even though I know the answer) because my talking is bumpy.'

EMOTIONAL RESPONSES

While often unable to verbalise internal feelings, the primary school pupil may well be experiencing a range of negative emotions associated with speaking. Children engaged in speech therapy describe a plethora of emotions – such as frustration, anger, embarrassment and fear – when asked to communicate their feelings about stammering. This cocktail of feelings would be difficult for an adult to manage and certainly demands a great deal from a young school child.

> *I haven't told my teacher because I feel too scared and I think it would make me feel better if I did. It makes me feel quite sad. Sometimes they try to help me in a bad way, like 'hurry up with your sentence'. Sometimes they think I'm making my stammer up.*
>
> *(Source: www.guardian.co.uk/education/2009/jun/30)*

Impact on construing of self

The impact of cognitive and emotional responses on how the pupil views himself is important to consider. Very often a child will move from an outgoing, confident preschooler to an older pupil who has less confidence in a range of speaking and social situations. He will begin to make choices on the basis of how much speaking there is in a situation and how fluent he predicts his speech will be based on past experience.

New opportunities may also be approached in a similar way, even though he has no previous examples on which to base his anticipation. He can decide not to do certain things, such as take part in group activities or speak out in front of others, because he is fearful of stammering and the reaction from others. In essence, he moves from a child who has 'bumpy talking' from time to time to a child who stammers.

Returning to the iceberg analogy described in Chapter 2, it is clear that this is a crucial stage in the development of stammering. An increase in awareness of speech disruptions can occur at this time either naturally or due to comments made by others. How the pupil responds to this awareness is very significant in the development of the 'under water' elements of the stammer. If he tries to modify his speech by forcing sounds out, this increases the overt component. On the other hand, if he attempts to minimise the occurrence of the stammer by changing target words and/or avoiding speaking, the stammer goes under ground and a covert component develops.

The alternative, more useful strategy involves a relaxed, accepting attitude. In this approach the pupil does not change his speech using force or struggle, but uses easier breathing and articulation methods. In addition, he does not compromise his communication and takes the opportunity to engage in new social and speaking situations.

Making this choice is not easy as the child will instinctively wish to increase the effort of speaking and want to avoid words and situations which are difficult and painful. It would be especially hard if those around him are encouraging him to speak differently and not to stammer. However, if he is in a supportive environment, the preferred option can become more possible.

It is curious how stammering is regarded in society. It would be an anathema for adults to criticise a child for using a wheelchair knowing the child was unable to walk. However, many adults will seek to change the speech of a child who stammers, for whatever reason, by instructing him to talk fluently. If stammering speech was generally more accepted by others, this would make it easier for the child to respond appropriately and more effectively to the onset of dysfluency in his speech. Paradoxically, this too would mean the stammer was less tense and less likely to develop a covert component.

Demands that might arise in primary school

Annual change

The structure of many primary schools is such that children in a class change teacher every year. While this has undoubtable benefits for all concerned, it does require each pupil to make a new beginning with a different teacher, adapt to a new regime and alter routines at the start of each academic year.

This can be daunting, especially for a pupil with a stammer, as the child is never sure whether his speech issues have been discussed with the new teacher. The pupil will be uncertain about the new teacher's approach to managing the incidents of stammering in the class, if and when they arise, or any reactions from class members.

Formal educational assessments

The assessment of a pupil's performance and abilities is of importance to teachers, and parents or carers. The child may be unaware of the ongoing continuous assessment carried out in the classroom but will know he has to complete formal assessments at key stages of his education. He will have picked up on how important adults believe these to be and can feel under some pressure to do what is expected of him.

Oral or verbal presentations

Once in primary school, a pupil will experience a greater demand on his expressive speech. He will be required to speak out in a number of informal and unstructured situations as well as some formal and structured ones.

Register

It is a requirement that a register of attendance is taken at the beginning of the morning and afternoon session in primary schools. The morning roll call can be particularly challenging as there are often numerous other classroom demands happening simultaneously: coats taken off and hung up, shoes changed, lunch boxes and water bottles collected, homework handed in etc.

Teachers handle these situations differently. Some require complete silence, others set pupils a task to do while the register is being taken (such as a word search or consolidation exercise for the previous day's work). Some teachers ask the pupil to make a set response when their name is called out, e.g. 'Here, Miss Smith', while others use it as an opportunity for the child to experiment with foreign languages, encouraging them to say a greeting in, for example, Spanish, French or Japanese.

Whatever the format, a pupil is required to respond to the teacher twice every day, usually in a particular order, in a short window of opportunity, with a verbal response and in front of his peers.

Learning to read

The ability to read is an important skill attained in primary school years. The process of learning to be a competent reader will require the pupil to read aloud to adults, usually on a daily basis. It may be the same adult but often would involve a variety, including the class teacher, classroom assistant, adult volunteer, parent or carer and, on occasions, a literacy coordinator and deputy or head teacher.

When reading aloud, the pupil is using a number of cognitive processes (i.e. identification of phonics, sound blending, visual and auditory comprehension) in addition to his speech motor abilities. In order to maximise opportunities to practice reading skills, a child may also be asked to read aloud to himself, with another pupil or in a small group.

Reading skills will be monitored by the class teacher and assessed formally at least once per year but usually more frequently. When carrying out an assessment, the teacher is required to make a judgement about the fluency of the pupil's reading. It can be confusing for the teacher to differentiate fluency in reading from fluency in speech. It may help if teachers refer back to the signs of stammering previously outlined, i.e. repetitions of sounds and syllables, blocking without sound on initial sounds of an utterance, disrupted breathing etc. This is different from hesitations before words without struggle and a pupil restarting a word to improve his blending or sequencing of sounds.

The key difference is that a pupil with a stammer will usually be experiencing physical (and emotional) struggle. Let's look at a specific example using the phrase 'Biff and Chip were going for a walk'.

Reading without fluency:

Child: *Biff and Chip wh-e-re* [child attempts sound blending) where –
Adult: [correcting] *Were.*
Child: – *go-go-going for a w-a-k* [child attempts sound blending], *wak, walk* [self corrects].

Reading with speech dysfluency:

Child: *B-B-Biff and Ch-Ch-Chip* [initial sound repetition of at least three iterations on names he can sight read] *were* [silent block before word] *going* [production of this word is forced or pushed out] *for a wwwwwwwwalk* [initial sound is prolonged].

A pupil with dysfluency will have more problems at the start of a sentence and/or after he has taken a breath. He will have difficulty with proper nouns and with 'information carrying' words, so he is more likely to stammer on 'going' and 'walk' than 'were' and 'for' or 'a'.

Of course one clear and transparent way of determining the nature of the pupil's difficulty is to ask the one who knows: the child himself. He will know what the issue was and, given the opportunity, will be keen that the teacher knows 'it was a bumpy sound/word' rather than 'I didn't know what the word was'.

Responding in class

In large group settings, a teacher will be monitoring a pupil's participation and noting if he does not answer questions. One teacher may target him and ask him a direct question to encourage and develop this skill. Another teacher could use methods that randomly select children to respond, for example names generated by the smartboard or selecting pens/wooden sticks with pupils' names on at random from a pot.

For a child who is anticipating dysfluency, this can be particularly difficult as he is not choosing when to speak nor what to speak about. He is not in control of speaking turns or talking topics.

At primary school I felt left out. I'd like to perform, especially with my different voices. When I started in Year 7, my maths teacher asked me a question and when I couldn't answer without stammering she thought I was taking the micky. I got a detention. It wasn't until my form tutor intervened that she realised it was true.

(Source: TES Extra for Special Needs, September 2005)

Asking questions

Primary school pupils are encouraged to critically evaluate materials and generate their own questions. For example, one science-themed class was observed experimenting with optimum growing conditions for broad bean seeds. The children were asked to work in groups and identify locations in their classroom that could be used to vary the amount, direction and intensity of light for the seeds, such as under the teacher's desk, in the stationery cupboard or on the window sill. They were required to consider the light in the class and ask the teacher about the locations they could choose for their seed pots. This work demanded much of their language skills: talking together, formulating and sharing ideas, and then discussing with the teacher before presenting their chosen locations, with a rationale, to the class.

Presentations and performance

Spontaneously speaking out loud in front of a class of peers is not usually as difficult as presenting information formally in the class or a school assembly, and certainly not as anxiety provoking as a Christmas or end-of-year performance. Several elements combine to make these communication situations the most demanding: having to speak at a certain time, saying particular words, being in the spotlight, feeling you are being judged and the perceived importance of the situation.

Levels of excitement

As adults we sometimes forget what an exciting place childhood can be. School life presents several situations in which the level of anticipation is raised. Simple events like having a visitor in class, a 'dress as you like' day, fundraising events like school fetes and so on are all examples where routines are changed and children play different, more exciting roles. Some primary schools also have opportunities for the older pupils to visit locations outside their locality and in some cases to go on residential trips.

For a pupil who stammers these 'exciting' times can mean an increase in anxiety related to speaking: new people to talk to, new topics and words to attempt to say, and further demands on controlling his level of fluency.

Relationships and classroom dynamics

Teachers report that primary school pupils are frequently falling in and out of friendships. Girls seem particularly prone to volatility in their relationships at this age and into teenage years. A girl can be friends with a particular individual at one moment then be a hated enemy the next. Disagreements may be over in a flash but can sometimes be prolonged and may involve other affiliated friends over time.

Boys, on the other hand, seems less volatile but can also have disagreements. A boy may brood over an argument for a while and then suddenly blow up into an aggressive altercation in the playground or sports field. However, a boy rarely holds onto a grudge for any length of time.

As relationships develop, the demands on each individual grows. The friendship will extend into home and leisure time; friends will be invited for tea, birthday parties, a sleepover, even a weekend stay or holiday. For a child who is dysfluent, this puts his speech under increasing pressure as he extends the circle in which he speaks. The friend may know and accept he has a stammer but what about siblings, friends of siblings, parents and relatives who he could meet during an extended stay? These may become issues that the child will need support in managing.

Bullying and teasing

Bullying and teasing is one of the most feared situations that any child anticipates. Often a child who stammers feels he is a likely target for such behaviour. In reality, if he has attended the same school for a number of years and grown up with the same group of peers it is unusual for them to change their behaviour towards him. However, a specific incident can spark an alteration in relationships or may be provoked by a new person or new dynamic in a peer group.

More often, bullying and teasing occurs when the pupil has not grown up with his peers. In this situation an acceptance of how he is and how he presents himself has not been established. A child who has to change schools, for example, may experience some negative responses to his stammering. This can be countered by particular personality traits and self-belief: the more confident and assertive the pupil is, the less likely it is that he will be targeted by bullies.

> *Annallie was a 7 year old who began to have difficulties coping when she moved house and started attending an independent school. In her previous school she had managed well, using age-appropriate language skills and controlling her dysfluent periods appropriately. However, her peer group in the new school were very articulate and assertive girls and Annallie's skills were no longer adequate. Consequently she struggled, both with her fluency and socially.*

Key points to remember

- Every primary child will experience significant social changes. A pupil who stammers at this age is no different. These social changes create demands on a pupil's communication skills.
- At this age, it is likely that the child has been stammering for some time. The stammer may well have changed, as will his awareness of it.
- There may be physiological changes in the pattern of stammering.
- The child can change how he responds to his stammer: he may feel differently about stammering. It may cause him to be anxious about some situations. He may decide he can no longer do certain things because he stammers. He may feel differently about himself as a result of his stammering.
- There are a number of demands on a pupil's speaking in primary school:
  - o   annual changes such as having a different teacher
  - o   formal assessments
  - o   verbal participation (including the register, learning to read, answering and asking questions)
  - o   excitement related to specific events
  - o   relationships and classroom dynamics
  - o   bullying and teasing.

5 Helping pupils who stammer manage the demands of primary school

Introduction

In this chapter, a number of practical ways to help a primary school pupil who stammers will be covered. These are divided into ways in which:

- the environment can be modified to help facilitate communication
- the teacher could change her communication or manage situations which happen routinely in the class
- the child himself can be helped directly
- a speech and language therapist might contribute.

There is obviously some overlap between these areas, but by looking at situations in this way the child's difficulties can be better understood and managed.

Stammering is a complex problem and as a result there is rarely one way to 'fix' it. The best way is usually a combination of:

- identifying the demands in any particular situation and
- helping the child increase his capacities to redress the balance.

No one stammer is the same and no child's response to his stammer is the same. Consequently, a management plan should be tailor made for each individual pupil.

As a general principle, speech and language therapists will use a 'least first' approach; an incremental programme that gradually introduces strategies to bring about the change required. So, for example, if changes in the speech rate of those *adults* who speak to the child result in the pupil being able to speak more fluently in a dialogue with them, then why teach the *child* to modify his speech? If, however, all possible environmental adaptations have been made and there is no change in the child's level of fluency, then more direct work on the pupil's speech would be appropriate.

The environment

To begin a management plan in schools, the focus should be on the school environment to ensure it is the best it can be to facilitate fluency in a pupil. It should aim to create a safe place to stammer: it is important that the pupil feels it is okay to stammer in the classroom and does not fear the implications of stammering. He needs to be able to speak openly and in as relaxed a manner as possible. He should believe that his efforts to talk will not be judged on the basis of his delivery.

To create such an environment, the teacher needs to show she is herself accepting of his stammer. This will be demonstrated by giving the pupil time to talk and showing no reaction to his stammer, either verbal or non-verbal. She should engender the same acceptance in the other children, managing any incidents of mimicry or teasing and certainly stopping bullying if it occurs.

There must be an openness about stammering. There can be taboos around talking about stammering in society, and lots of misunderstandings about what it is and how a person experiences dysfluency. In schools, a dialogue needs be established between the pupil and his teacher or other adults in the classroom. Very often the individual himself has ideas about his speech, such as what makes it difficult and what makes it easier. The pupil may need help to express these thoughts and feelings and to then be heard by important adults who will help him manage his difficulties productively.

The teacher

As indicated in the previous section, the teacher plays a crucial role in fostering the best possible classroom environment for the pupil to manage his speech. In addition, there are specific things she can do that will help.

Model a slow rate of speaking

When speaking to the child in a one-to-one situation, the teacher should demonstrate a low rate of speaking. This is one way in which the demand in communication is reduced by:

*   providing time for the child to process information
*   indicating that communication does not need to be rushed
*   modelling a speaking rate that the child could use.

This may be a little more difficult than it seems. How do we speak more slowly? There are a number of factors that influence the rate of a person's speech. First there is the speed of articulation, which is how quickly the tongue, lips, jaw etc. are moved. By slowing down the speed of the articulators, a speaker can slow down the length of time it takes to articulate the sounds of a word.

A second way to speak more slowly is to increase the number and duration of pauses that punctuate speech. A speaker will pause before speaking to compose an utterance, take time to breathe, and pause to think. By increasing the length of these silences and/or by introducing more of them into an utterance, the time taken to speak is increased. So a teacher can use a slower speaking rate with a pupil by slowing her articulation rate and/or by increasing the number of pauses before or during her sentences. The pupil may be able to tell the teacher which method helps him best.

Create an appropriate window for the pupil to speak

Creating an appropriate window for the pupil to speak is especially important when a child has processing problems that underpin his dysfluency. A teacher often does this as a matter of course in the classroom: where a pupil is not able to answer a question, a teacher may say she will come back to him after asking two or three other children. This gives the pupil time to think and enables him to get his ideas together and compose a response.

It can be a useful process for a child who stammers. However, it is important that the teacher does not keep him waiting too long before returning for his answer. A long wait will increase the anxiety and anticipation he has over his response and create more problems than the initial processing difficulty. It would be useful if the teacher asks the pupil what would be most helpful: 'Would you like more time?' 'Shall I come back to you after I've asked Lauren what she thinks?'

In addition, the pupil with dysfluency needs to feel he will not be interrupted during his response or have his turn hijacked by others. The anticipation of someone taking his turn can cause him to increase his speaking rate in order to get his message out as quickly as possible before any interruption. The teacher's role, therefore, is to enforce the discipline of appropriate turn taking in the classroom so that every pupil is allowed to finish what he wants to say and not be interrupted or have his sentences finished off by others.

React appropriately when a pupil stammers

One question speech and language therapists working with children who stammer are frequently asked is: 'What should I do when a child stammers when talking to me?' Adults often feel that they do not know the rules when it comes to reacting appropriately to stammering.

The key reactions relate to non-verbal behaviour. First it is important to keep soft eye contact. Some adults think looking away is the appropriate action when a pupil is stammering. However, this breaks the communication and can indicate to the child that his behaviour is embarrassing and not to be observed.

Second, having a relaxed body posture helps the pupil feel relaxed and shows that he is being listen to. Not indicating anxiety or embarrassment is also crucial, and it goes without saying that smirking or laughing is totally inappropriate.

When the pupil is struggling badly to get his word out, a sensitive acknowledgement of his difficulty is often helpful, along the lines of: 'I can hear you are getting really stuck on this word. However, I will wait for you to say it and I won't interrupt or say it for you unless you want me to.'

Establish a supportive dialogue

Having experienced a severe disruption in the child's speech can be useful: it provides a reason and a chance for the teacher and pupil to have that important conversation about speaking and to address the ways in which it can be managed in class.

The dialogue should include the pupil's experience of his stammer: the when, where and how as described in Chapter 3. The teacher should also try to establish how the individual feels about talking when different demands are asked of his communication – when answering questions, reading aloud etc. In addition, it is important to see if the child has ideas of his own on how best his speaking problem can be managed in these situations.

If there are no specific ideas from the pupil, then the teacher may offer her ideas based on experience of what helps children communicate. For example, she could find out which type of question is most useful: open-ended options ('Tell me about the story'), directed questions ('Which character did you like best?') or forced alternatives ('Was it a happy or sad ending?')

Perhaps the key objective for this conversation is that the pupil is clear about what is expected of his speaking: he *will* be asked to speak out so his classmates see him treated equally, but *will not* be judged on the basis of how fluent or dysfluent he is. What matters to the teacher is his contribution, not the manner of his delivery.

Finally, the teacher and pupil can take the opportunity to negotiate the nature and timing of both overt and covert support that the teacher might provide. The pupil can help the teacher know when and if she should 'step in' to help him and what she might say to him and the rest of the class (if appropriate) if he becomes severely blocked or stuck. A non-verbal signal can be usefully employed here.

Use praise

It can be a natural reaction to congratulate a normally dysfluent pupil for speaking fluently. However, the result of this discriminatory praise is to convey to him that his fluency is valued above all else.

In order to counter this perception, it is recommended that teachers give more general praise in respect of the pupil's general communication. Comments on communication should include non-verbal behaviours, the content of his utterance, the expression or the feelings conveyed, his clarity and volume, and the precision and fluency of his articulation, regardless of whether he has spoken fluently or not.

Do not ask the pupil to change the way he speaks

Asking the pupil to change the way he speaks – for example saying: 'Stop. Take a deep breath. Speak slowly' etc. – suggests to the child that his speech is wrong and he needs to change it. Giving a catalogue of suggestions in this way is also confusing and does not necessarily equate with why he stammers: does stopping really help? Is his breathing shallow? Is his rate too fast? Do any of these factors impact on his fluency?

Manage difficult situations

The teacher should discuss with the child the situations in which he appears to experience more stammering. She needs to know how best to help the pupil manage his fluency most effectively, and that includes knowing where this happens most often. As there is no one answer, the simplest solution is to ask the individual.

Teachers are mostly sympathetic and give me the time I need. I have a good way of dealing with registration. When my form teacher calls my name I reply, "Es, ma'am', which should be 'Yes, ma'am'. If you say it fast you can't hear the missing 'y'. I often know the answer in lessons but I avoid putting my hand up. If a teacher asks me directly and there's a short answer, I'll say it. If it would mean a long explanation, I'd say I didn't know.

(Source: TES Extra for Special Needs, September 2005)

If a pupil has no ideas immediately, here are some options from which he could choose and possible actions to help him.

Register

- Reorder the register to put his name second or third so he does not have to wait too long to answer.
- Rather than have a set response, let children choose how to respond. Alternatively, some teachers have introduced responding with 'hello' or 'good morning' in different foreign languages. Each pupil is encouraged to experiment with using a different one each day, or the same one if that is more comfortable. Any child may also bring some new ones to add to the list of options and for everyone to try.
- Have an activity (e.g. a word search) for the class to complete while the register is being taken. This takes the focus off the responses and will help the pupil feel his response is not being listened to.
- Invite the class to make a non-verbal response to the register, such as putting a hand up or standing up in their place. This may take a little longer but can help the pupil who struggles to answer and, as a by-product, may enable the class in general to settle down and be silent.

Queues

- A pupil who is dysfluent can find queues especially problematic. There are several factors that contribute to the demand in this situation: having to wait, anticipating stammering, having to say a specific word or words, feeling rushed (because others are waiting behind them), feeling listened to and judged, and perceiving that the listener has not got time to wait for them or listen long enough for them to get their words out.
- If the pupil reports that dinner or other similar queue-based situations (e.g. boarding the school bus) are giving rise to anxiety, it is worth informing the relevant school staff of the issue. The teacher or speech and language therapist can meet them and give advice on how to react to the child appropriately. (The advice would be similar to the section earlier in this chapter on reacting appropriately – see page 45.)

Answering questions

- Ask the pupil direct questions when he has indicated that he is able to answer them. This indication may be as simple as when he has his hand up or in response to a cue previously agreed by the pupil and the teacher.
- Avoid asking him at random. The fear of being asked at any time in a discussion can be greater than the fear of being asked at a specific, agreed time.
- If asking the class in turn for a response to a question, don't leave the pupil who is dysfluent waiting a long time. It is better to ask him as second or third responder.
- If you have asked the child a question and he is struggling to formulate his response, allow him time to compose his answer. Tell him you will ask someone else and then come back and find out his answer. This is an appropriate response if you believe the pupil has not been able to formulate his reply.

If, however, he has an answer but cannot say the words he wishes to because he is stammering, stay with him and let him finish; in this case, telling him you will come back to him is likely to increase his anxiety over the difficult words. He might also use any additional time to choose a different response or change his words in order to make a response easier. Neither of these strategies are useful for him to learn and may compromise his ability to say what he wants to say in the longer term.

It is very difficult for a teacher to differentiate between a pupil who has processing issues as opposed to one who does not but is stammering over a word. The solution is to ask the pupil to tell you the nature of the problem. A teacher can ask the child directly: 'Are there words in your answer that are hard for you to say or is it that you need more time to think of your answer?' In this way the teacher is clear and can make the most helpful response.

- Divide the class into pairs and ask for responses from them, but watch for equal participation within the pair. A pupil who is dysfluent may rely on his partner and opt out of offering his ideas.

Asking questions

- Create time and space when the pupil can come and ask you or another staff member a troublesome or important question. This may be at the beginning or end of a session, or at some time when he can speak while not being observed by other children in the class.
- The teacher may need to allow the pupil to ask a question at a less-than-ideal time. An individual who stammers can have a sense of being able to speak at a specific time: he may therefore use that opportunity to ask a question because at that time he feels he can. Sometimes it can appear that he is being inappropriate or impolite but it is probably neither. Rather, it is the child seizing an opportunity to speak when he feels he has the control and capacity.

Reading aloud

- Let him take his turn early in the reading session or choose for himself when to take his turn, so he is not waiting a long time.
- Avoid having children read a paragraph each. The pupil who is dysfluent will have calculated which will be his paragraph and will be reading it while others are taking their turn. He will be worrying over particular words within the section and generally not taking in the content of sections being read by others.
- Reading in pairs is less challenging so can be used to reduce the demand on the pupil. Make sure you know who he is most comfortable being paired with: there may be some children who he feels are more critical of his speaking ability and with whom he is likely to experience less fluency.
- Reading in unison with one other person, as a group or as a whole class will be easier for the pupil who stammers than reading alone.

Verbal participation/performance

- Always include the pupil who has a stammer in class or general school performances. Do not presume that he will not wish to play a part. Many adults who stammer remember being excluded from such activities. They go on to describe how they took this as an indication that their stammer was 'very bad' and/or that they were not good enough to be included.

- Provide a number of options for the pupil which are graded by the level of demand placed on speaking. For example, a main speaking part would of course be the most demanding, whereas a single utterance (word or sentence), saying something alongside/in unison with another child or holding up a sign with words on it would be the least demanding. Let the individual choose the most appropriate level for him.

- Rehearsal time is often a feature of school performance. The pupil with a stammer would benefit from practising his speaking part in the environment in which it is to be delivered, rather than in the classroom. Hearing your voice in a class or assembly hall can be helpful to know how loud it needs to be and how slowly you need to speak to be clearly understood. A teacher or assistant can provide valuable feedback to assist the pupil in determining these factors and give him confidence in his performance.

The playground

- Children who stammer frequently report problems with bullying or teasing in the playground, cloakroom or toilets. Obviously these are locations where the presence of teachers or other adults in authority is less apparent. It has proved useful in some schools to assign 'buddies' to pupils who may be at risk of unwanted attention from specific groups or from older children. A buddy is a trusted individual who will look out for a particular child and 'be on his side'. The buddy also facilitates the reporting of any untoward incidents to an appropriate teacher, should that be required.

The child

Children attending the Stammering Support Centre in Leeds were surveyed to determine what they considered the least and most useful things teachers could do to help them in school.

Least helpful were:

- *being told to hurry up*
- *being told to speak more slowly*
- *being picked on to answer a question.*

Most helpful were:

- *being asked if they want to answer a question*
- *being told to take their time and knowing the teacher would wait*

> • *the teacher saying: 'If you ever need support, come and talk to me whenever you want to.'*
>
> *Those surveyed also said they would like teachers to know about stammering and what it is like to live with a stammer.*

As stated at the start of this chapter, it would be unusual to ask a teacher to teach a pupil direct controlling strategies as a first step. The usual approach is the 'least first' option, even within child-centred approaches, where small changes are introduced to improve the child's speech and his ability to cope with stammering.

In early primary school these first steps with the child might include the following.

Talk about talking

Much importance is given to helping the pupil discuss his thoughts and feelings about stammering. The aim is to prevent or reduce any negative responses to the episodes of stammering and to encourage a relaxed attitude to it.

Strategies to encourage relaxation

Relaxation techniques are useful, such as simple mindfulness techniques that focus on quiet, slow and rhythmical breathing and the 'breathing square' (see Figure 5.1). The breathing square consists of breathing in for three seconds, holding for three seconds, breathing out for three seconds and holding for another three. As the child is able to control his breath more effectively, the length of time for each 'leg' of the square can be increased to five or up to seven seconds.

A teacher could use these strategies with a pupil who appears anxious when speaking and/or shows signs of disrupted breathing when speaking. The techniques should be introduced to the child as an individual, with visual aids to help him understand and retain the concept. In the case of the breathing square, he could be encouraged to

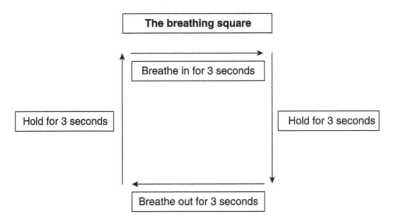

Figure 5.1

move his finger along the length of the lines while breathing to give him a sense of the time to be taken.

Focus on other communication skills

Sometimes a pupil can become so focused on speech fluency that he forgets the other skills that are crucial in effective communication. Gently and occasionally reminding a child to keep eye contact, maintain an upright, relaxed posture, look calm and at ease, and to not fidget is advice that will help him understand the holistic nature of communication.

In addition, aspects of speaking such as volume, clarity and appropriate expression can usefully be developed at this age.

Manage time pressure

A pupil will be aware of time pressure on his speaking responses. He will have noticed the teacher and other children waiting for him to talk. He will know that he has a certain window within which to speak and that sometimes other children and adults fail to allow him to complete his turn: they interrupt and his turn is lost.

These issues will put pressure on him to get out what he wants to say as quickly as he can, before he loses his turn and before listeners notice he has stammered. Work can be done on two levels to help the pupil deal with this problem.

1.   Create an environment where he is unlikely to have his turn taken by another speaker and where he knows that others will wait for him to finish speaking.
2.   Help him to manage the feelings of pressure he may be experiencing and which will cause him speak when he can (which may not always be at an appropriate time) and to rush. Encourage him to take the time he needs to compose his response and deliver it clearly and at an appropriate time, so all can appreciate what he has to say.

> *People tell me to hurry up, but I get annoyed because I speed up and then I stammer more, so then it takes even more time to get the words out.*
> *(Source: Michael Palin Centre for Stammering Children)*

Manage emotional responses

A teacher should be aware of how the pupil feels about his speech. Establishing a dialogue with him to explore this has already been discussed. If this conversation reveals significant negative feelings relating to his speech, specific speaking situations or his levels of confidence in these situations, then the teacher and her staff can use this information to develop a plan to help the pupil change these feelings.

A plan to develop self-confidence could include the use of praise for non-speech activities, such as tidying up after a class activity or playing imaginatively. It could also include helping the pupil develop a role in class that helps build his confidence (e.g. having a role to integrate a new class member or conveying messages to the school office, initially with the support of another child or with a written message as back-up).

Encourage the child to be an advocate

It is very useful to help the pupil talk openly about his stammer. This role has several benefits: the subject of stammering becomes acceptable to talk about and not a taboo to be covered over, the child's peer group come to understand it more fully, and the individual himself is empowered in the process. Once stammering becomes an open topic and is understood, the pupil is less likely to fear stammering in front of others. The relaxed attitude to stammering that he needs is therefore more likely to be achieved.

Speech and language therapist

A speech and language therapist may well have been involved with the child and his family from an early age. Chapter 8 will describe the management plan that the therapist would usually employ. However, it is useful to summarise briefly what her role might entail with a primary school pupil. The therapist will:

- provide information to the family and school staff on communication skills, stammering and its development
- involve and educate significant other people in the child's life about stammering and how to respond appropriately when the child stammers
- identify key factors in the child's environment that disrupt his fluency and manage these factors to reduce their impact
- with a younger primary school pupil, use a behaviour modification programme to increase the use of fluent speech
- with an older primary school pupil, introduce some fluency strategies and teach the child to use these in a gradual way
- encourage older pupils to meet others who stammer, reducing their feelings of difference and helping them develop support networks
- discuss with the pupil the appropriateness of formally educating the class about stammering. This could involve the child himself or, more often, might be a presentation that the therapist gives to the class about stammering.

Key points to remember

- The environment should be a safe place to stammer and a place where stammering can be discussed in a way that helps the pupil feel at ease, not uncomfortable.
- The teacher can contribute by:

  o   modelling a slow speaking rate when talking to the pupil
  o   creating a window of opportunity for the pupil to speak and not be interrupted
  o   reacting appropriately when the child stammers
  o   establishing a supportive dialogue
  o   using praise

    o   avoiding telling him to change the way he speaks

    o   managing situations that are difficult.

- The pupil can be helped to manage his speech, his thoughts and feelings about stammering so that they do not undermine his general communication and academic performance.
- The speech and language therapist can play a role in educating others about communication and stammering, developing speech and psychological strategies and a support network for the child.

Top tips: How to help a primary school pupil who stammers

- Create a safe place to stammer.
- Encourage an openness about stammering.
- Slow down your own rate of speech when talking to the pupil.
- Monitor and regulate the number and type of questions you use in order to reduce the verbal demand on the pupil.
- Count to five silently before responding to a child's question to slow down the rate of turn taking.
- Avoid interrupting or speaking at the same time as the pupil is speaking.
- Do not complete his words or sentences in an attempt to minimise the stammer.
- Speak to the pupil using sentences that are shorter in length and use vocabulary that is age appropriate.
- Listen more and talk less.
- Use praise and compliment the child on his general communication skills.
- In class, make sure the pupil has his turn and is listened to.
- Use choral and paired reading as appropriate when reading aloud.
- Respond to instances of dysfluency in a calm, reassuring and accepting manner.
- Establish a supportive dialogue.
- Avoid telling the pupil to change the way he speaks.

6   The demands of secondary school for pupils who stammer

Introduction

There are so many developmental, emotional and relationship issues emerging in adolescence that it can be difficult to identify what is having the most impact at any one time. Looking at stammering in adolescence poses the same problem: it can be hard to know what factors are contributing to the level of dysfluency.

In this chapter the various demands that could be significant will be described. Readers will note that these demands are not unusual and are typical of the experience of any young person. However, how a pupil who stammers reacts to these demands may well be different and impact greatly on his communication in school.

This chapter will take a pupil perspective, describing the important changes in the pupil's development and his stammer during these years, and noting key behaviours teachers should look out for.

> *When my words don't come out easily my mouth sometimes changes shape. I screw up my eyes and go red. Then I get terrible butterflies in my tummy, as I feel I won't find a way out. I try and get over the problem word but then another will get stuck and another.*
>
> *I often stop talking and take a few breaths to calm myself. I close my eyes as well while doing this; I don't like to see people's reactions. Mostly it works, but sometimes people lose interest or run out of time. They try and finish what they think you were saying.*
>
> *I stammer more if I'm talking to someone I don't know, less with my family and friends. I never stammer when I sing or am speaking in different voices I've invented.*
>
> *(Source: TES Extra for Special Needs, September 2005)*

Adolescence is often thought of as the transition period between childhood and being an adult. Each young person will experience a range of physical, cognitive and emotional changes during this time. Physically he becomes more like an adult, and changes in his physiology may mean he is less coordinated, less focused and eats a great deal and more often!

His cognitive and intellectual development also take major steps towards adult processes. He develops the ability to be rational, although may not always choose to use this new-found skill. In addition he can reflect on his own and others' behaviour and make good attempts at coming to useful conclusions about them. He is able to use adult language structures and, with the appropriate opportunity, is able to learn foreign languages. His vocabulary of his native language expands to include more technical and specialist words. He also uses different language 'codes' for different people or groups. Many adolescent groups, especially males, have nicknames for peers, words for items and phrases to signify certain things that may not be recognised outside the group. This helps to identify members and aid group cohesion.

Emotionally he will consider himself to have moved on from childhood, but in many ways still needs the support, balance and grounding that adults can provide. He will begin to engage in more meaningful, intimate relationships with others. However, friendships can be unpredictable and there may be periods of falling out within and among groups of teenagers. On the other hand, there is often excellent peer support for individuals experiencing problems. The peer group begins to exert even more influence than in previous years. It becomes a source of validation for the individual, who strives to maintain an appropriate role and be accepted by members of the group. Social media plays a significant part in establishing the individual's place and contributes to group dynamics.

There is much oscillation between child and adult roles; one minute a young person will demand freedom and want to dissociate himself from the family or adult input, and in the next moment he will need advice and help to manage a particular situation. The teenager wants to have the freedoms associated with being an adult but appears reluctant to accept any of the responsibilities.

During these years the young person will be trying to identify the core constructs that make him who he is. He will be asking the question 'Who am I?' in different ways and in different situations. In trying to answer this conundrum, he may well experiment with a number of adult-type activities, such as using alcohol and misusing substances, engaging in extreme diet or physical regimes, or trying out new and different leisure activities – all to see what happens and how the results relate to his identity.

The stammer

It is probable that any pupil attending secondary school who has a stammer will have been dealing with this speech problem for several years. Generally the older the stammer, the more likely the specific behaviours will have become habitualised and the whole problem compounded by negative thoughts and feelings.

The stammer may have become more overt (i.e. development of the top part of the iceberg), with increases in muscle tension and struggle behaviours. Alternatively the stammer may be less observable but the features below the waterline will have increased, leading to negative thoughts, feelings and compromises to the person's ability to live his life in the way he would like. In some young people both these options occur, with an increase in both overt and covert features happening over time.

Changes in the stammer

Young people with an overt stammer

For a young person with a more overt stammer there may be a number of distinctive features of stammering at this age.

- The easy word and sound repetitions characteristic of early years will have been replaced by more forceful – and possibly lengthy – repetitions of sounds and syllables.
- There can be significant prolongations of sounds, which again often include tension and struggle-type behaviours.
- Blocks – some prolongations may be silent with articulation locked and vocal chords closed, resulting in no sound being produced.

> *Sometimes I want to say something and I can't say a single word, so people around me wouldn't even know that I'm trying to talk, and by the time I get it out they'll have moved on.*
> *(Source: www.guardian.co.uk/education/2009/jun/30/stammer-stutter-school)*

- Breathing can be disrupted, either before speaking (with rapid and/or multiple intakes of breath) and/or during speech (with loss of air or running out of air).
- Some individuals develop associated or concomitant behaviours. Examples include tapping of the feet or hands, changes in body postures, fidgeting, eye closure, blinking, and facial distortions or grimaces. These behaviours result from attempts to disrupt stammering.

> *Josh would bang his knee with his hand and stamp his foot during a speech block. He did this once out of frustration and to his surprise it stopped the block and he was able to say the word. Subsequently he used it purposefully to release his speech. The effectiveness of this behaviour soon wore off but the habit remained and became an integral part of his stammering behaviour.*

- Postponement behaviours – in an attempt to start speech, some individuals use fillers such as *ers* or *umms*, other speech sounds (e.g. *mmm, aaa*), starter words (e.g. *actually*) or phrases (e.g. *what I mean, you know, the thing is*). These utterances provide fluent 'run ins' for sounds or words that the speaker anticipates having difficulty saying. As with associated behaviours, they can become part of the stammering behaviour if used frequently.

Young people with a covert stammer

For a young person with a more covert stammer there may be a number of other responses to stammering at this age.

- Negative emotions – in research with adults, suffering was the primary theme in an analysis of their stories. Four key elements of suffering were identified as helplessness, shame, fear and avoidance. Similarly, young people report these strong feelings before, during and after stammering.
- The experience of stammering and these associated negative thoughts and feelings impact directly on how the developing young person feels about himself. As previously stated, this is at a time when identity is being questioned.

Harriet thought she was unattractive to others because of the way her face sometimes became distorted when she stammered. She isolated herself from her peers and was very unhappy as a result.

Features shared by both

Some features may be relevant for both overt and covert forms of stammering.

AVOIDANCE

This is a very significant feature of persistent stammering. It is the individual's attempts at reducing the occurrence of overt or open stammering and comes in a number of forms.

• **Sound or word avoidance** – a young person may be fearful of saying specific sounds or words because he has past experience of stammering on them. Consequently, he will avoid words that start with the problem sound and avoid saying difficult words.

  Avoidance is usually in the form of word substitution. The replacement word may be similar or close to the meaning of the target word. However, in some cases he may use a word chosen at random because he can say it fluently. This may be confusing for the listener as it can appear that the individual has responded inappropriately, gone off track, lost focus and/or introduced a different topic for no apparent reason.

  Sometimes a young person may choose not to speak at all to avoid saying words he fears.

Layton had a severe stammer and attended speech and language therapy for regular support. Teaching staff at his school, however, were puzzled by the fact that he was receiving speech and language therapy as he was fluent in class. There was some suggestion that perhaps Layton came for therapy to avoid participation in certain lessons.

The therapist arranged to visit the school to observe Layton's participation in class and discuss the apparent mismatch of speech behaviour in the different settings. During the observed lesson Layton was chosen to answer a question and did so without difficulty. Later he was asked another more complex question but on this occasion he said he did not know the answer.

Following the lesson, the teacher and therapist discussed his performance in class with Layton. The teacher analysed his performance; she said his first answer showed he had no problem speaking out in class. His lack of response to the second question was understandable and due to the complexity of the answer required.

> *Layton was then asked how he saw his participation. His explanation was different from that of the teacher. He said that the fluency of his first answer was because he did not anticipate any problem with the words required. However, the second answer, which he knew the answer to, contained several words which would cause him to stammer so he chose to say he did not know the answer. He knew this made him look less intelligent than he was, but preferred this to the alternative of giving the right answer but stammering while doing it.*
>
> *Such behaviour could lead to a lowering of academic expectations by both Layton and his teachers.*

- **Situation avoidance** – in this instance the person with a stammer will fear the communication demand relating to a specific situation. Examples include a play reading in drama class where he would have to read out a character's lines of text, or a maths class where the session focuses on mental maths with answers provided verbally and often very quickly by pupils. In both of these examples, it is not the specific words that are the issue but the context in which the person has to speak.

  Avoidance at this level would involve the young person finding excuses not to place himself in the situation. Letters may be written by parents to explain absences, or the individual may feign illness or absent himself for some other reason. Some pupils have deliberately acted inappropriately in an attempt to be excluded from the lesson rather than face the fear of speaking.

- **Feeling avoidance** – stammering can be associated with the expression of some feelings. For example, the stammer can be more pronounced when a person is angry, upset or experiencing another strong emotion. Where a young person is aware of the link between his stammer and an emotional experience, he may choose not to express the emotion at all. Alternatively, he will 'dampen down' or suppress his emotions when trying to control his fluency.

  Paradoxically, the reverse is also true: a person may experience more fluency at times of heightened emotion. Some pupils have deliberately become angrier in a situation in order to be more fluent. This of course is not an avoidance of feeling but a manipulation of feeling to enhance fluent speech.

- **Relationship avoidance** – relationships can create a number of speaking demands. When a person meets or is introduced to a new individual he would usually say his name. A person who stammers can find that very difficult. In establishing and maintaining friendships, there are additional speaking demands. Individuals will phone each other and converse on a regular basis. The phone can be problematic for a person who stammers.

  Meetings inside and outside of school may be arranged during which the young people will usually converse freely. Once again conversations in public places which may be noisy or in which it is difficult to be heard will challenge a person's ability to be fluent.

Taken as a whole, the outcome of these well-used and complex avoidance strategies may be good levels of fluency, but at a price. The individual will be compromising his communication, not saying what he wishes to say and not speaking when he wishes to. It may lead him to make important choices on the basis of avoiding stammering rather than on his academic ability. For example, a pupil may opt out of foreign language learning as soon as he can because of the demands on his verbal skills, even though he may be very competent and enjoy the subject.

IMPACT ON CONSTRUING OF SELF AND ROLES PLAYED

Sometimes an individual discovers that he is more fluent when he uses a funny voice, tells a joke, or makes an aside or a quip. Swearing may also be something he finds he can do fluently. In an attempt to keep himself as fluent as possible, he may well do more of these things. Thus he becomes a different type of communicator: the joker in the class, the one who makes quick-witted comments at the expense of others or the abrasive individual who frequently uses bad language.

SOCIAL AND EMOTIONAL ISSUES

Adolescence can be a difficult time for any young person but having a stammer makes it especially challenging. A teenager wants to be recognised by his peers and accepted as one of the group. Having a stammer, however, sets the pupil apart from his peers and potentially marks him out as the focus of teasing or ridicule.

A young person can feel the need to hide his stammer and may be reluctant to put himself in situations where it will be obvious to others. As a result he can seem less approachable, less spontaneous and in some way socially different. At worst the adolescent who stammers can become a loner, isolated from his peers, and may have thoughts and feelings that resemble depression. Indeed, there are pupils who have had suicidal thoughts as a result of their experience of stammering at this stage of their lives.

Checklist of questions for teachers to consider

How a young person understands or construes his stammer at this age is crucial to its effective management. For this reason, a checklist of questions for teachers to use as the basis for a constructive dialogue with an individual pupil is useful (adapted from Stewart and Turnbull, *Working with Dysfluent Children*, Speechmark, 2007).

Checklist of questions for teachers to use as a basis for dialogue with pupils

- Does the pupil construe himself in terms of stammering? Does he think that how he speaks is more important than what he says? If he makes an interesting contribution in class but stammers, is he embarrassed by what he has said?
- Does he construe other people or other situations in terms of his own stammering, e.g. *He made me stammer* or *I always stammer in English but never in maths?*

- Does he believe that his peers and teachers construe him predominantly in terms of his stammer? Does he regard his stammer as a part of his identity that he thinks others are most aware of and concerned about?
- Does he make decisions that are based on stammering? For example, does he make subject choices at school which demand little speaking and opt out of studying those that demand more as soon as he is able to do so?
- Does he blame his stammer for a poor performance, e.g. *If I didn't stammer I'd be the best in my class at French*?
- Does he appear to have a sense of resignation about his speech, feeling that whatever he or anyone else does, nothing will change?
- Does he have a 'don't care' attitude to his stammer or deny that it concerns him in any way, when the evidence suggests otherwise?
- Is he a loner? Does he keep his feelings to himself? Conversely, does he seem to become angry or aggressive easily?
- Does he seem to construe himself as different from others? Does he seem isolated from his peers or appear out of place within his peer group?

Demands that might arise in secondary school

Transition to secondary school

The move from primary school to secondary school is a great source of anxiety for most pupils and subject to a number of stressful myths among year groups. 'Big school' represents a transition from the safe dwelling of known surroundings of primary school into a totally different education environment. The pupil loses the familiarity of one classroom teacher and one classroom of friends and peers, and has to cope with numerous teachers, their different teaching styles and changing groups of peers. Initially his old friendship groups will be disrupted as he mixes with different peers in different situations. He will be introduced to new subjects, new learning regimes, new work demands and new speaking situations.

Generally this transition is handled with excellent collaboration and sensitivity between the schools involved. There are usually visits to secondary school to get acquainted with some of the year group, the geography of the school, the teachers and the timetable.

However, the specific needs of a pupil who stammers are not always identified and managed appropriately. Sometimes their anxieties can relate to specific situations about which fluent speakers will have no concerns. Following are some statements that a teacher can use as a basis for a conversation with a pupil who stammers who is moving to secondary school.

Conversation prompts for pupil transitioning to secondary school

When I stammer this is what you might see/hear ...

When I stammer this is what you might not be able to see and hear (i.e. thoughts and feelings and things I do to avoid stammering) ...

Talking in school

When I read aloud in class . . .
   When I have to answer the register . . .
   When I answer questions in class . . .
   When there is a group discussion . . .
   In subjects where there is speaking out (e.g. foreign languages, English,
drama) . . .
   When I have difficulty speaking it is helpful . . .
   When I have difficulty speaking it is not helpful . . .
   In secondary school I am looking forward to . . .
   In secondary school I'm a bit worried about . . .
   I would like teachers to know . . .
   I do not want teachers to know . . .

Calum was worried about the move to secondary school. He had been to visit the school he was to attend and had met his head of year and some of his subject teachers. However, he was still anxious and getting physically upset when talking about it at home with his mother.

During a visit to his speech and language therapist, the issue was raised in the context of demands that might be made on his speech. Calum was asked to identify his biggest worry with regard to his stammer. He said he was anxious about getting on the bus and asking for his fare when there might be older pupils who he did not know on the bus and they would hear him stammer. The implications of this for Calum were that the situation would provide fuel for teasing or bullying in other settings at school.

Calum's worry was subsequently taken by the therapist and Calum to the school. It was discussed with the learning support teacher who was able to identify where the older pupils caught the bus. She then showed Calum an alternative bus stop that he could use to catch the bus before the older pupils got on.

Annual changes

There is unlikely to be continuity in all pupil groups. Although some schools operate a house system or tutor groups that have the same composition throughout an individual's stay at secondary school, most pupils will still experience several changes each year, for example changes in the configuration of classes for different subjects and changes in teachers for specific subjects.

This means that once again the young person will face the demand of speaking in front of new groups of peers. Many of them will not have progressed through primary education with him and are therefore unlikely to know about his stammer. He will be fearful of their reaction, individually and collectively, and, in his worst-case scenario, unsure how a teacher might manage any incidents of mockery or ridicule. He will also have concerns about his new teachers and their style of teaching, especially their way of asking for verbal responses in class.

Unlike primary school, this set of anxieties will be repeated at the start of each new academic year when classes and subject sets are reorganised.

Oral or verbal presentations

Once in secondary school, the young person will experience a greater demand on his expressive speech. In primary school the language level required was much simpler; the answers tended to be straightforward. However, in secondary school the aim is for pupils to work out their own understanding and opinions, and to articulate these ideas verbally in a logical, often concise way.

There may be added requirements in some subjects for presentations to follow a recommended format, with stated aims, an introduction, a middle and a formal ending or conclusions drawn. Other subjects that focus on creativity may be more fluid and encourage self-expression. In addition, pupils may be encouraged to experiment with different modes of delivery and to convey their ideas with, for example, dynamism and authority.

The pupils will be asked to engage in verbal activities in pairs, small groups and in class discussions. Group work can be problematic and needs to be well managed. Some individuals with a stammer have reported 'hiding' in group activities and going along with the ideas of dominant group members rather than proffer their own opinions.

If a young person feels that his speaking is already compromised by stammering, school may be a very stressful place indeed. But there are also some specific oral or verbal situations that can cause particular anxiety for the young person who stammers.

Register

Taking the register continues to be part of secondary school routine. However, it is required to be taken at the beginning of each lesson rather than the twice-a-day routine of primary school. Missing the register can trigger certain responses. For example, if a pupil is absent for two lessons, many schools would then ring home to enquire about his absence.

Some teachers have a more relaxed approach to this demand than others, choosing to start pupils off with an activity as soon as they enter the class and take the register more informally while the young people are occupied. For other teachers it acts as a way of settling the class down and lessons only start once it is completed.

There may also be other situations in which a register is taken in secondary school. For example, a house system operated in one school and each house met once a week for a house meeting. The register for house members was taken at the beginning of the meeting by the senior prefect and was a very formal situation.

As in primary school, if the pupil who stammers feels the silence of the class and the ears of his peers attuned to his response, then the demand on his fluency will be great. The more relaxed the approach and the more flexible the response he is able to make, the more he will be able to cope.

Reading aloud

At secondary school age, a pupil is usually competent in reading. However, the demand required in secondary education is significantly different from that in primary. The pupil will discover that there are occasions when he is required to read aloud as the subject or teaching style of the teacher demands. Unlike primary school, textbooks in secondary education may not have been assessed to match the reading levels of the pupils. There may be a situation in which the text is above the reading ability of an individual.

This will obviously create a significant demand for the pupil. Although his reading competency will no longer be formally assessed, it will remain an activity that causes the young person much anxiety. He will be aware of having to read the text as it is written and will not be able to use any avoidance strategies (e.g. word switching or reordering of words in a sentence) that he might employ when speaking spontaneously.

If the teacher asks that the class read in turn then he will experience anxiety as his turn approaches. This will absorb and distract him and he will lose his ability to concentrate on the content of the text. If the paragraph or portion of the text he is to read has previously been identified by the teacher, he may well practice his 'turn' while others are reading.

He will also be anxious if the teacher is choosing pupils at random to read aloud. Young people who stammer have reported employing a variety of strategies to get out of these situations. These include not turning up for a lesson where they know reading aloud will occur, feigning illness, and disrupting the lesson by behaving badly in order to be excluded.

Responding in class

In large-group settings, a teacher will attempt to create an environment in which speaking out is encouraged but also managed in order to facilitate a pupil's engagement with the lesson material.

Teachers have different styles and will approach participation in different ways. For example, a foreign language teacher described modelling the target verbal response several times himself, then asking more confident pupils to make their response. Less confident or able individuals would be given notice that they would be required to respond, enabling them to prepare and plan.

A teacher will notice if an individual does not participate in discussions and may well target him specifically by asking direct questions. Multiple questions and/or questions requiring a detailed, sequential and complex answer are the most demanding for any pupil. However, an individual who is dysfluent will have the added issue of anticipating blocking or repeating initial sounds in his answer. Once again the stress will be related to the stammer being heard by peers and the teacher, and the fear of judgement and ridicule as a consequence of this.

Asking questions

Secondary school pupils are encouraged to critically evaluate materials and generate questions. Inference and prediction are key components that teachers will be looking for in a pupil's understanding of texts and information. For the individual, asking for clarification is a crucial aspect of learning. If he feels unable to check his understanding or ask for further information, then his learning may be significantly affected.

> *Thea was in a maths lesson. The teacher was explaining sine and cosine and Thea was not clear about the concept. She was feeling left behind in the activity but did not feel able to ask the teacher questions in front of her peers because of her stammer. So she started messing about with her friend Karen and together they decided to opt out of the lesson. She told the teacher that Karen was feeling a bit dizzy and needed some fresh air.*
>
> *Thea never caught up on her learning of this area and ended up failing her maths GCSE which she had the ability to pass.*

Teachers have said that on occasions pupils ask questions to control and distract a teacher from the aims of a lesson. One teacher even describes it as a 'type of sport'. As such, pupils will be aware of the power their questions have within the classroom. Although this sort of behaviour cannot be condoned, a young person who is dysfluent may not be able to engage in this dynamic and therefore may feel separate from his peers.

Specific subjects

Subjects that were not included in primary school may be a cause of concern for a pupil who stammers. Foreign language learning, drama and other lessons in which verbal participation forms a central part are likely to cause the most anxiety. For example, up to a third of the assessment of foreign language competency is carried out through speaking tasks. Pupils will be able to prepare their answers to a set of questions in advance; however, a proportion of the assessment is spontaneous answers to unknown questions. A pupil's interaction and fluency in the language is also assessed, which again raises the question of whether or not the teacher, assessor or moderator is able to distinguish between the fluency of language and the fluency of articulation.

It is recommended that those assessing fluency refer back to the signs of stammering previously outlined in Chapter 2: repetitions of sounds and syllables, blocking without sound on initial sounds of an utterance, disrupted breathing etc. This will differ from the hesitations that a pupil may experience while formulating a sentence or finding a vocabulary item: an individual with a stammer will usually be experiencing physical (and emotional) struggle.

In addition, the place and occurrence of the disruption to fluency will be generally predictable in a young person who stammers. He will have more dysfluency at the start of a sentence and/or after he has taken a breath. Proper nouns and 'information carrying' words will also be more difficult. The pupil will be acutely aware of why he is having a problem, so if there is any doubt it is worth taking the time to have a conversation with him and ask about the nature of the dysfluency. For example, the assessor might say: 'I notice you had some trouble saying *xyz* and I am curious to understand if it was because of the French/German/Spanish, or whether your stammer got in the way. Why do you think it was difficult?'

Rather than a demonstration of verbal skills, there may also be occasions in other subjects where a pupil has to give an oral presentation to demonstrate his learning. These scenarios will be particularly difficult for an individual who is dysfluent. While preparation and planning time will help him control the content of his presentation, he will not feel he has control over the reactions of others should his fluency break down.

When choosing the academic subjects he will study to GCSE standard, he may well have considered the amount of speaking each subject requires. It is vital that teachers are aware that this can play a significant part in his decision-making process. Conversations at the time of subject selection should always be carried out with the knowledge of how much speaking anxiety a pupil has in a specific subject. This must be discussed openly and the pupil given the appropriate information regarding the allowances made within the various exam board regulations for those who have speaking difficulties.

Presentations and performance

Formal presentations will be one of the most challenging situations that a dysfluent individual faces. As in primary school, a number of elements combine to make this difficult: having to speak at a certain time, saying particular words, being in the spotlight, the feeling of being judged and the perception of the importance of the situation. At secondary level there may be additional factors related to the complexity of the content and the use of visual and computer technology to enhance the presentation.

Some presentations may be given in groups. This provides an opportunity for a pupil who stammers to take a non-speaking role, such as operating the computer or managing some other visual aid for the presentation. While this can be appropriate for a younger child, it can be used as an avoidance strategy for an older pupil. It can mean that he never takes the opportunity to play a speaking role. This can cause later complication when, given a different subject, a higher year group and an exam requirement where he has to present verbally, he has no experience on which to draw.

Many verbal presentations are assessed by teachers, either informally or formally, and on occasions may be recorded for further assessment by external moderators. All of this puts expressive speech under significant pressure.

Formal educational assessments

Assessments occur at key points in life at secondary school. Apart from ongoing informal assessments and year-end exams, GCSEs, AS and A levels are important markers of a pupil's education. The outcomes of these exams remain on his record, and help determine how his education and employment will progress in future years.

All secondary school pupils are aware of the significance of these assessments and respond to the pressure that they bring in different ways. For a dysfluent adolescent, the stress will increase with worries over the speaking components of any assessments he has to complete, for example assessment of his conversational speech in a French oral or a monologue in drama.

There are specific adjustments that can be made and guidance produced by the Joint Council for Qualifications. Details of these adjustments and how a school can ensure a pupil accesses these arrangements are given in Chapter 7 (see page 81).

Relationships and classroom dynamics

As described earlier in this chapter, adolescence is a time when the young person begins to have more meaningful, intimate relationships with his peer group. Early secondary school years appear to engender feelings of social vulnerability and threat in a young person who stammers. These dissipate as he progresses through the year groups. By the time he is at the upper end of the school, many threats have subsided and the individual is often more confident.

Relationships in these years can be volatile, with intense affection on the one hand and intense loathing on the other. The unpredictability of teenage relationships is often commented on by parents, who find it hard to keep up with who is friend and who is foe at any one moment. Friendships and the strength of feeling that result can be a factor that upsets an individual's level of fluency. Similarly, being 'in the group' or excluded from it for whatever reason may contribute to poor levels of speech control in a young person.

On the positive side, peer support also has an effect. Where the adolescent is supported by the group or an individual he relates well to, this can be a means of helping him to manage his speech and the negative feelings he may experience from time to time.

Talking to authority figures may also play a part at this age, affecting a pupil's level of fluency. The communicative demand is increased when talking to a person in authority or a person perceived to have authority. There are many authority figures in secondary school, ranging from the head and her deputy to departmental heads, year heads, form teachers and prefects. Conversations with such people are likely to involve the authority figure leading the conversation, a question-and-answer or interrogative style of interaction, and the young person being required to supply information.

The pupil will be aware of these demands and may try and avoid situations involving senior staff where he can. He may decline to take messages to senior members of staff, avoid random meetings with certain senior teachers and/or enlist the help of other pupils in any necessary dialogue.

It is impossible to describe adolescent relationships without mentioning the role that social media plays. Contact with peer groups and extended friendship groups is continuous in these years. It often appears that the young people are unable to function without the contact that social media allows. In a recent experiment reported in the media, a group of adolescents were invited to abandon social media for a week. Only a small percentage of them were able to complete the experiment. For the others, they reported not knowing how to fill their time and found the disconnection too great to manage. For an individual who stammers, social media has provided a useful non-verbal and acceptable way of making and maintaining friendships without openly stammering.

Bullying and teasing

Bullying and teasing are more likely to happen in secondary school, especially in the early years. These are the times when the pupil is most vulnerable, has not established his role or identity in the peer group, and may be identified as a target by older pupils. Such scenarios often occur where there is reduced or limited adult presence: at break times, entering and leaving school, in locker areas, changing rooms, dining halls, toilets and the school bus.

A pupil with a stammer will be aware of the possibility of teasing as he makes the transition from primary school. It is a subject that can be discussed with the relevant school staff at an early stage. This gives the pupil the confidence that he knows how to cope with it himself, who to talk to about it, and how the school as a whole manages incidents when they occur.

Key points to remember

- Pupils who attend secondary school are likely to have been stammering for some time.
- The pattern of the stammer will have become established.
- Features may involve aspects of struggle and tension.
- Covert features are also likely to have been incorporated into the stammer, including avoidance and negative thoughts and feelings.
- The stammer can impact on how the pupil feels about himself, and thus his social and emotional well-being.
- There are a number of demands that can arise in secondary school which increase the communicative demand on the pupil:

  o   annual changes to class composition and subject teachers
  o   oral and verbal presentations, including the register, reading aloud, responding in class, asking questions, presentations and performances
  o   some subjects have greater demand on speaking – such as English, drama and foreign language learning – but other subjects occasionally include presentations. Pupils may make their choice about studying subjects based on the amount of verbal presenting they have to do.

- Formal assessments and examination requirements for oral presentations place demands on an individual who stammers. Various allowances can be made for such pupils (see Chapter 7).
- The volatility of relationships during the adolescent years can affect the level of fluency they experience.
- Bullying and teasing are a frequent feature of school life reported in the early years of secondary school by many pupils who stammer.

7 Helping pupils who stammer manage the demands of secondary school

Introduction

This chapter describes a number of practical ways for teachers and others working in a secondary school to help an older pupil who stammers. These are divided into ways in which:

- the environment can be modified
- the teacher and pupil can determine ways to facilitate communication and develop useful skills and strategies
- specific difficult situations can be managed.

As stated in Chapter 5 on primary-aged pupils, there is no one way to manage stammering. Once in secondary school the pupil will have been stammering for some time, and the problem is likely to be compounded by negative thoughts, feelings and unhelpful avoidance strategies. In order to manage what has become a complex problem, the management will need to consist of helping the young person to:

- reduce his sensitivity to stammering
- reduce struggle behaviours
- reduce his negative thoughts and feelings,
- prevent or reduce his avoidance behaviours
- develop an attitude of openness to stammering
- develop useful fluency controlling strategies
- minimise any effect stammering has on his construction of himself, his confidence and self-esteem
- implement a management programme across a range of difficult situations.

How this is implemented will depend on the young person and his environment. A speech and language therapist will tailor make a programme to fit the pupil's needs. Secondary school staff will be involved in many, if not all, of these aspects and especially in the reduction of environmental demands, in a similar way to those discussed at primary level.

The environment

In this section the nature of the school environment and aspects of the teacher's interaction that can best facilitate fluency will be outlined.

Create a safe place to stammer

One of the aims of intervention with a secondary school pupil is to foster an openness about stammering. This will help the process of 'lowering the waterline' on the metaphorical iceberg. In this way the individual will reduce his negative thoughts and feelings, his struggle behaviours and his sensitivity to stammering.

Being open about stammering in the classroom is crucial to achieving this aim. There are two components to this:

- a pupil feeling able to discuss the issue of stammering
- a pupil being able to risk stammering in front of the class without fear of judgement, criticism or ridicule.

Model acceptance

All school staff have a responsibility to promote an environment in school which is accepting of each individual. The class teacher will be accepting of difference, especially with regard to the verbal contributions of pupils, irrespective of the way in which they are expressed. She will model how pupils should listen to others, again especially with regard to different verbal presentations.

Establish ground rules

In managing difference, the teacher will set ground rules for the class on how to behave and demonstrate tolerance. This of course will apply to all aspects of the pupils in a class: race, ethnicity, religious beliefs, gender, as well as disability or impairment. It can be an important lesson for this age group and stammering should not be excluded.

Any examples of intolerance must be managed within the established ground rules of a class – consistently, swiftly and in an even-handed way. Incidents of mimicry or teasing and bullying must not be tolerated or condoned.

There should also be a set of ground rules relating to how everyone communicates in the classroom. This will include the discipline of turn taking, with pupils and teachers waiting and listening while others are speaking. In this way everyone will have time to speak and be allowed their full turn, with interruptions frowned upon.

Young person as advocate

Talking openly about stammering is a powerful way of helping a young person become less sensitive to stammering, managing any avoidance and negative thoughts and feelings. There are a number of situations in which this is appropriate.

Informally, a pupil should be encouraged to talk about what stammering is, what it feels like to stammer and the impact it has on him. This could be to staff members in the school, including receptionists and kitchen staff, and small peer groups as appropriate. Such informal talks need to be set in a relaxed environment and listeners should come with a stance of curiosity rather than morbid fascination.

In a more formal setting, a pupil might carry out a survey in school and talk about stammering as a topic for a class presentation. Speech and language therapists often try and involve children and adults who stammer in presentations about stammering. Sometimes they give talks that have an educative function or in some cases as part of a fundraising campaign (e.g. for the British Stammering Association). The narrative of a young person who stammers is often a moving account of managing adversity and can convey more to an audience than a therapist can.

The teacher

Secondary school pupils who stammer report that some teachers are easier to speak to than others. A teacher can adopt a particular communication style that facilitates an optimal level of fluency in a pupil. The key factors are outlined in the following sections.

Use calm, unhurried speech

When talking, do not reply quickly to questions that are asked. Pausing and counting to five seconds silently before answering shows pupils that verbal responses do not have to be rushed.

A teacher can also work on speaking at slower rate (see Chapter 5, page 44). To summarise briefly, a teacher can slow down the speed of the movement of her articulators (i.e. tongue, lips, jaw) and/or increase the number and duration of pauses that punctuate her speech.

Be an active listener

When listening to the speech of a pupil who stammers, the teacher needs to be an active listener, using good eye contact, maintaining a relaxed, still posture and having a calm, relaxed manner. She should also summarise and paraphrase the content of a pupil's contribution and seek to clarify the contribution as appropriate. This demonstrates that her focus has been on the content of what has been said rather than the delivery.

Demonstrate tolerance and acceptance

If the pupil stammers when speaking, the teacher should demonstrate her tolerance and acceptance of his speech. She should keep eye contact with him and not look away or avoid his gaze, in order to keep the channels of communication open. The pupil who stammers may look away but the teacher should keep her gaze on him in a non-confrontational, supportive manner.

She should maintain a relaxed posture, stay calm and wait patiently. She should not attempt to hurry him or interrupt his turn and fill in the word he is struggling with. The exception to this would be if she has previously negotiated with the pupil that this was what he wished her to do when he was having severe problems with his speech.

After the contribution she might comment on the content of what has been said. She would rarely mention the stammer. However, in exceptional circumstances when the dysfluency has been significant, she might recognise the difficulty and praise the effort if it was appropriate, for example by saying: 'Thanks, Zain, for that comment. I realise that was difficult for you but I'm really glad you stuck with it because it is such an important point you have made. What Zain has enabled us to realise here is . . .'

Have supportive dialogue

As in primary school, a dialogue needs to be established between the pupil and his teacher or other adult in the classroom. It is also important to set this in motion for the start of his transition from primary to secondary education. The dialogue should explore the young person's experience of his stammer, perhaps using the stammering iceberg as an illustrative tool. Discussion of what goes on under the waterline will help the teacher and pupil uncover any negative thoughts and feelings and unhelpful strategies, such as avoidance behaviours.

The teacher could also ask the pupil about particular situations in school when different demands are made on his verbal communication, e.g. register, answering questions, reading aloud, class participation, group work, giving presentations and performance. In addition, it would be important to see if the young person had his own ideas or previous examples of strategies that worked well and helped him cope. If the pupil suggests using avoidance or other less helpful strategies, it is important for the teacher to discuss with him why these ideas are not helpful in the long run.

An example of a structured conversation that can be used during the transition from primary to secondary school can be found in Chapter 6 (see page 60). Another structured conversation for use at key stages or the beginning of each year is included here.

Helping me to speak in school: the pupil's view

---

1. Talking in class

When I have to talk in a group or pair in class I usually . . .
When I have to read out in class I usually . . .
When the teacher asks me a question in class I usually . . .
When I answer the register I . . .
When there is a class discussion I usually . . .
When I have to present something in class I usually . . .
If I don't understand something in class I usually . . .

---

2. Subjects / teachers

The easiest subject for me to talk in class is . . .
The hardest subject for me to talk in class is . . .
The class/subject in which I need most help with my speech is . . .
My stammer is likely to affect my exam results in subjects(s) such as . . .
The easiest teacher to talk to is . . .
The hardest teacher to talk to is . . .
My stammer will affect my choice of options for GCSE and A level
   because . . .
The teacher who understands the most about stammering is . . .

(Continued)

(Continued)

---

3. Managing stammering

Stammering affects my school life because . . .
When I stammer in class,   teacher A usually . . .
    teacher B usually . . .
    teacher C usually . . .
When I stammer in class my friends usually . . .
When I stammer in class kids I don't know so well usually . . .
When someone is trying to help me with my speech they usually say/do
. . .
Apart from in class, I also stammer in situations such as (e.g. break time,
dinner queue) . . .
The best way teachers can help with my speech is . . .
The best way my friends can help with my speech is . . .
The best way I can help my speech is . . .

The key objectives for the teacher in this conversation are again to enable the pupil who stammers to have an understanding of what is expected of his speaking; that is, that he *will* be asked to speak out but will not be judged on the basis of how fluent or dysfluent he is. What matters to the teacher is his contribution, not the manner of his delivery. This would be the same as assuring a pupil that the content of his writing was important, not the quality of his handwriting.

It would be useful to repeat this type of conversation at the start of each academic year to see if there have been any changes, new speaking techniques learnt, or any new anxieties around different teachers, subject sets or other situations. In addition, a discussion at the point of choosing options for GCSE and A levels is vital to ensure that judgements are not overly influenced by the young person's view of his stammer and its impact on his verbal expression.

Paul, an adult who stammers, was asked to comment on his experiences in school, including what was helpful and what was unhelpful. 'I had very few bad experiences at school. I could read aloud in class and be fluent a lot of the time. However, with hindsight some things would have helped me.' Paul went on to list:

- *teachers talking to him about his stammer and finding out how it made him feel and behave*
- *teachers having a basic understanding about stammering*
- *teachers explaining his situation to other pupils*
- *teachers encouraging him to be more involved in lessons through question-and-answer sessions*
- *teachers encouraging him to pursue subjects and further education that interested him, rather than choosing them because they involved minimal speaking.*

'Being more open about my stammer and how it affected me was perhaps the biggest lesson I needed to learn. I doubt teachers in the 1950/60s were equipped to help me achieve this. Hopefully, teachers today would be better able to help me be more open about my stammer and find ways to deal with it in the classroom.'

Supporting communication

At primary school level it is recommended that teachers do not try and change the way a pupil speaks unless under the direction of a speech and language therapist. The situation in secondary school is somewhat different as the pattern of dysfluency is likely to be well established. At this point it is useful to develop and encourage a young person who stammers to use good communication skills. Examples which would be relevant to non-fluent pupils are:

- keeping their head up and maintaining good eye contact, especially during stammering
- having a relaxed, still and confident body posture – pupils who stammer may use movement and fidgeting as a strategy to get out of blocks or other dysfluent episodes, but this can be distracting for a listener who will find it difficult to focus on the content of what is being said
- developing good non-verbal skills, such as facial expression and use of appropriate gestures.

By praising a dysfluent pupil's overall communication skills, he will come to understand that fluency is not the only aspect and certainly not the most significant skill of good communication.

Support social skills, especially conversation

Some young people who stammer have reported being so focused on their level of fluency that they have difficulty thinking about the social and pragmatic skills that their peers use naturally. A pupil who stammers may benefit from support with a number of conversational skills including:

- how to start a conversation, including introducing himself
- how to keeping a conversation going by maintaining a topic, asking others appropriate questions, and knowing how and when to change topic
- being aware of and understanding non-verbal cues from his listener
- how to end a conversation in a timely and appropriate way.

Manage speaking anxiety

A pupil may experience high levels of anxiety when anticipating speaking. The anxiety may be so significant that it prevents him from making his contribution. In order to help a pupil keep this to a minimal and a manageable level, he should be asked for his response early on and not be kept waiting. The teacher and pupil could negotiate that if he has his hand up he will be asked immediately or as the second person to answer.

If he has not indicated he wishes to respond but the teacher wants to encourage or develop his understanding, then she can prepare him to make a contribution, for example by saying: 'OK, some of you have not got your hands up to answer so I'm going to give you a bit of time to think about this. Let's go through it again. Then, Emma, I will come to you first, then Zac, and then Stephen.' In this example the dysfluent pupil has not been singled out but is part of a group being given time to think of their responses, thus the young person is supported and simultaneously treated the same as other class members.

The breathing square described in Chapter 5 is also a useful technique to manage anxiety and can be taught to secondary school-aged pupils as appropriate.

The pupil who stammers may also experience feelings of needing to speak when he can: he can feel that he has an opportunity of fluency at a specific time. This could be an optimal time or an inappropriate time, such as when others are speaking or when there is an enforced silence. It might appear at these times that the individual is flouting the ground rules and/or behaving rudely or badly. It is important that the teacher or other member of staff discuss these occurrences with the young person and establish whether or not this behaviour is related to maximising his fluency. If it is then other more appropriate strategies should be introduced to enable the individual to adhere to the class ground rules.

Look out for avoidance behaviours

Avoidance is a very significant feature of persistent stammering and is common at secondary school age. The young person, seeking to hide the overt features of his stammer, will employ a number of avoidance strategies: word, situation, relationship and feeling avoidance behaviours. These avoidance behaviours were detailed in Chapter 6; in this section, some specific behaviours associated with the avoidances will be described so that teachers can be aware of what to look out for.

WORD AVOIDANCE

- The young person may avoid giving a specific answer in class even though he knows it is correct.
- His communication might appear unusual at times as he chooses an inappropriate word or appears to lose track of what he is saying or change the topic in a random fashion.
- Alternatively, he can be the quiet pupil in class who is not a problem, says very little and few members of staff have heard him speak at all.

SITUATION AVOIDANCE

- A pupil who is always late for the register may be deliberately trying to avoid having to answer.
- There could be a series of unexplained absences for certain subjects where there are verbal demands being made, such as having to give a presentation or reading out a text.

- Sometimes disruptive behaviour is an attempt to be excluded from a lesson rather than facing speaking out and stammering in front of a peer group.
- As mentioned before, a pupil may choose his GCSE and A level options on the basis of the verbal demands and his experience of fluency rather than his academic ability.

FEELING AVOIDANCE

- An individual can appear passive and unemotional because he knows that his speech fluency deteriorates when he becomes emotionally upset or angry.
- Alternatively, he may use his experience of increased levels of fluency when he is very emotional. A pupil who flies off the handle and becomes angry for little or no reason might be deliberately using this behaviour so that he has greater fluency in the situation.

RELATIONSHIP AVOIDANCE

- Sometimes an individual who stammers can find himself outside the peer group. He is not deliberately excluded but, because he finds speaking difficult, he chooses not to engage with his peers in some specific social situations (e.g. using the phone, using Skype, meeting up in noisy environments). If the individual is not open about his speech difficulty, this can be interpreted as odd or different.

Develop self-confidence and self-esteem

Adolescence is a time when an individual's feelings about himself are significantly challenged. If he is not validated by his peers or does not experience situations that are self-validating, he may feel unconfident and possibly become depressed.

Interestingly, one teacher commented on the role that extra-curricular group activities have in this regard. A pupil who is part of drama, music and/or sports groups such as rugby, football, netball or hockey is able to establish himself as part of a peer group that consists of members outside his particular year group. This can give him a status that helps establish him in a school and contributes significantly to his level of confidence and self-esteem. If a pupil who stammers can be encouraged to participate in such groups, this may help him feel better about himself and find his place in school.

Another option is to give the young person some type of responsibility. Often a pupil who has appeared the most timid in his first few years can act as an effective buddy when he is older for younger, less confident pupils. This is a validating role for him to play. It can build his confidence in terms of his ability to make a broader range of relationships, including those outside the peer group.

Support fluency and fluency skills

One of the features of stammering, described in Chapter 2, is the variability and frequently unpredictable nature of stammering. The pupil who stammers will be acutely aware of this, sometimes on a morning-by-morning basis and even before he has spoken!

He may use this to his advantage and speak more on those days when his fluency levels are at their best. A teacher, too, can use it to get the best responses from the pupil. She may ask more of him on those days when she observes or the individual reports he is having a good day, and be less demanding on the days when he is less fluent.

> *Amelia and her French teacher had negotiated a way of indicating how her speech was on a particular day. She had a planner with a number of coloured dividers in it. On good speech days she would open the planner to show the green divider and on particularly challenging speech days she would show the red divider. In this way she indicated to the teacher the level of participation she could manage.*

Another solution is to negotiate directly with the pupil. The teacher could use the questionnaire earlier in this chapter as a basis for a conversation to establish where the individual needs support and what form that support might take. The teacher should work on a step-by-step approach, gradually increasing the level that is demanded of him over time.

A specific subject teacher can negotiate with the pupil to agree the nature and timing of both cueing and/or covert support that she or a learning support member of staff might provide. Principles of how and what to do when he stammers can be established. If he is learning specific fluency controlling techniques, then subtle cues or reminders for him to use these ways of speaking might be usefully included. A speech and language therapist could advise on what and how this would work.

> *Ollie was learning a technique called easy start or easy onset with his speech and language therapist. He had established proficient use of the technique in the therapist's clinic room, with her receptionist and had even tried it outside in a local cafe near the clinic. It was now time to try it in school.*
>
> *The therapist went to school and met with Ollie and his English teacher to discuss how this could be implemented. It was agreed that if he was struggling on a word when reading a text aloud and had forgotten about his easy start technique, the teacher would clear her throat as a prompt for him.*
>
> *This worked for a couple of weeks after which time Ollie told his teacher that he felt able to remember to use it himself in reading and did not need any prompting. The prompts were discontinued in reading but used occasionally when he got stuck while making spontaneous contributions in class discussions.*

Establish a support network

For younger pupils it can be helpful to have a buddy or mentor, perhaps from an older year group. However, such a practice should not set the individual out as having special needs, but rather as a strategy routinely used to support newcomers and help them integrate into school life.

On occasions a secondary school has been able to introduce pupils who stammer from different year groups. (In a school of 900 pupils, the research would suggest there will be nine individuals across the age ranges who stammer.) This interaction can be especially useful where a younger pupil meets someone coming to the end of his school life. In this instance the older pupil is able to reassure and support the younger one and help them feel less anxious and more confident.

Let staff know

A key management strategy that is frequently mentioned by pupils who stammer is the need for staff to know about their speech difficulty. A member of the teaching staff, usually the learning support teacher, should take responsibility for communicating with the pupil's individual teachers about his speech. This will include his particular anxieties and needs in specific subjects and how his stammer is to be managed. This process should be repeated at the beginning of each academic year and if any changes occur during the year.

The special needs coordinator will liaise with the young person's speech and language therapist and ensure that the school are kept up to date with any management programme that is being implemented. Chapter 8 describes the various types of programmes that may be carried out.

Provide support information

The individual and the family should be given information on other support organisations for individuals who stammer. Of particular relevance is the British Stammering Association who have information for different age groups on all aspects of stammering. They also provide information for schools and have an education officer to answer specific queries. See the resources section at the back of this book for more information.

Manage difficult situations

Should the pupil who stammers be asked to contribute to the same extent as other pupils in the class? Or should the individual be allowed to opt out or be excluded or omitted from participation to avoid embarrassment?

On one hand, forcing a pupil to do something difficult that could potentially humiliate him and cause him extreme anxiety and upset seems unnecessary and indeed unhelpful. On the other hand, granting him special privileges and making allowances that identify him as different could result in teasing from his peers and cause him to lose confidence in his own abilities.

There is no easy answer to this dilemma. As with all aspects of stammering, the solution should be negotiated with the individual and tailored to suit them. It may be that, in order to participate to the same extent as his peers or in a way the situation demands, he needs to have some capacities and strategies in place. Obviously these should be taught first and reach a level of competency appropriate for the situation. Once this is established, the pupil should be encouraged to implement these skills gradually over time.

If the teacher is of the opinion that the pupil has the necessary abilities but lacks confidence, she can negotiate a programme to develop his confidence, targeting the specific situation.

As with primary school age pupils, it is recommended that the teacher discuss directly with the individual situations in which he appears to experience more stammering. If he has no ideas immediately, here are some options from which he could choose and possible actions to help him.

Register

Measures to help a secondary school person who stammers during registration include the following.

* Reorder the register to put his name second or third so he does not have to wait too long to answer.
* Rather than have a set response, let the pupil choose how to respond. This may be a verbally or non-verbally.
* Have an activity for the class to complete while the register is being taken. This takes the focus off the responses and will help the adolescent feel his response is not being listened to.

Other situations in which the pupil has to say his name – such as introductions at the beginning of a new class or introductions to new teachers, new class members, visitors etc. – will also cause the individual significant anxiety and difficulty. As the young person cannot use word substitution in this situation, he is very likely to get stuck and experience significant levels of dysfluency.

The recommendation here is to encourage the pupil to be open about his stammer and introduce the stammer alongside his name. For example: 'Hello. Before I tell you my name, I need to explain that I have a stammer. I often get stuck saying my name so just give me a bit of time and I'll get there.'

This can be difficult for a young person as it involves being open about their difficulty. A teacher may need to support the pupil to do this and perhaps take a graded approach with smaller steps, for example being open with one person, then two or three friends, then a small group and so on.

Queues

A secondary school pupil who is dysfluent will find queues especially problematic. The same factors are involved as with younger children: having to wait, anticipating stammering, having to say a specific word or words, feeling rushed (because others are waiting behind them), feeling listened to and judged, and perceiving that the listener has not got time to wait for them or listen long enough for them to get their words out.

It is important to discuss with the pupil which queuing situations are the most difficult. If he identifies dinner queues, for example, then it may be necessary to talk to the relevant staff and where possible provide appropriate information on how best to manage the issue for the pupil. The speech and language therapist is a useful resource for such a situation and can meet with staff and give advice on how to react appropriately.

Verbal contributions in class

No adolescent likes to be singled out to answer questions in class in front of his peers. The same applies to a pupil who stammers. In fact, he is likely to experience significantly more anxiety in such a situation than a pupil who does not stammer. Putting a young person under this pressure means the teacher is unlikely to get the best response from him. The preferred approach would be to invite responses and ask him directly when he has indicated he has an answer.

When the teacher wishes to explore his understanding and needs to assess this through a verbal response, she should choose an optimal time. This would be in one-to-one interactions or small-group settings, on days when his fluency appears to be at its best, and on other occasions when he himself has indicated to her that his is able to risk a response.

If the pupil is indicating he has a contribution to make, the teacher should not have him wait for a long time before asking him to speak. The longer he has to wait, the more anxious he will become and this will affect his fluency.

The teacher should also be aware of the effect that complexity has on stammering. Recalling the demands and capacities model (see Chapter 2), the greater the complexity of language required, the greater the demand on the speaker and his fluency. If the pupil is required to explain something very complicated, perhaps involving a number of sequences or a topic that he has only recently understood, it is likely that this will challenge his ability to be fluent.

In such a scenario, the teacher can help by breaking the required response down into smaller segments. She may direct the pupil to give a response relating to the first few parts of the sequence or part of the topic, rather than the whole. This would be particularly helpful for younger secondary school pupils.

Another factor to be aware of is time pressure. If the pupil is asked to speak within a set timeframe or if he feels he only has a small amount of time to respond, this will impact on his level of fluency. The teacher must create the opposite effect and enable the young person to feel he has plenty of time to make his response and that he will not be interrupted or hurried.

Asking questions in class

A pupil may choose not to clarify his understanding of an issue rather than risk stammering in front of his classmates. The teacher must make it clear to him that there is always an opportunity to check his understanding with her individually at the end of a class or at some other agreed time.

Reading aloud

While reading is not assessed in secondary school in the same way as in primary school, it may still be used as a tool in the classroom for looking at information or exploring texts. For a pupil with a persistent stammer, reading can be an area of great concern. Because the words are fixed and other pupils know what he is expected to say, he is unable to use the strategy of word substitution without this being identified.

The most helpful tactic a teacher can use is to discuss reading aloud in class with the pupil. She can give him prior warning that this is going to happen and explore with him how best his participation can be managed. It may be possible to arrange reading groups of three or four pupils to make the situation less threatening.

Another option is to give the pupil prior warning of the particular text that is going to be read before the lesson. In this way the individual can have a look at it, prepare, and perhaps even identify a section that he could manage to read most confidently.

If there is no opportunity to prepare ahead of time, then the young person will generally prefer not to have to wait for their turn. However, the teacher should have discussed this with the individual and found out what his preference is rather than assume she knows.

Reading in unison or in a pair will be easier for the pupil and could be considered in some contexts.

Verbal presentations / performances

Giving presentations is often a feature of some subjects, such as English and drama. In addition, presentations may be used by teachers to demonstrate pupils' learning and develop their communication skills. It is a difficult task for a pupil and one that often causes anxiety in both fluent and dysfluent speakers.

However, some pupils who stammer will find that they are more fluent when playing a role, so it is important to discuss the activity with the young person and not over-protect him or single him out as different.

There are ways to enable him to get the best out of his speech.

- Discuss with the pupil how best to manage giving a verbal presentation. Having lived with stammering for so long, he may well have ideas of his own based on his past experience.
- Reduce the group size. If possible, have him present to one other person, ideally a friend or someone who he feels comfortable with and trusts.
- Promote the use of visual aids for all pupils. Not only is it a useful skill to have but it also takes the focus off the verbal aspect of a presentation. This will help the pupil who stammers feel that his speech is not the centre of the audience's attention and consequently enable him to be more relaxed.
- If the presentation is done by a group, make sure that in the preparation his con-tribution is listened to. The young person should feel able to negotiate his part in the group presentation. Often an individual will opt to take a non-speaking role, perhaps operating the slideshow or using a flip chart. Such a role will enable him to develop confidence in standing in front of the class. However, at some point he needs to be supported in making a verbal contribution.
- On occasions a class or tutor group may be required to present to a year group, assembly or larger number of pupils. Once again it should not be assumed that the young person who stammers will be unable and/or unwilling to take part. If he is treated differently from his peers, this contributes to feelings of low self-esteem and affects his confidence. A teacher can discuss the options with him, find out if he wishes to be included and, if so, what part he would feel comfortable in taking. This might be limited to the preparation or the development of the visual aids but may include some verbal contribution alongside another pupil or even alone.

If he feels able to take a speaking part, it is recommended that he practises in the place where the presentation will be given. The teacher or another staff member can give him feedback on his volume level and general vocal projection. She can also suggest ways of enhancing his non-verbal communication, which he might not have considered.

Oral exams

To ensure that pupils who stammer are not penalised during oral exams, 'reasonable adjustments' can be made. This follows recommendations made in the Equality Act 2010. Such adjustments would apply to the speaking component of specific subject assessments such as English and modern foreign languages, and include being given extra time.

In order to qualify for these adjustments, the school needs to apply to the exam board and provide evidence of the pupil's difficulty. Certain formal educational assessments (such as those demonstrating slow or delayed processing) and/or medical reports can be used as proof of a pupil's disability but may not be enough.

The board may require evidence of 'substantial and long term' difficulty. In such a case the school may use evidence collected over a significant timeframe, perhaps several academic years. This will prove a history of need and demonstrate what provision has been put in place to establish a normal way of working to support the pupil.

Zac had to do a verbal presentation as part of his GCSE English exam. He was very anxious about it and worried that his stammer would prevent him from getting a word out. His speech and language therapist met with Zac and his teacher to discuss what could be done to make the situation easier for him while still complying with the exam board's requirements.

The therapist came to school on the day of the assessment. Zac practised his presentation in front of her in a quiet classroom over lunch. She gave him feedback on his communication skills and volume. She also reminded him to use a couple of fluency-enhancing techniques he had previously learnt with her.

The assessment then took place. The teacher and one of Zac's friends came and observed, along with the therapist. Zac's friend helped him relax before he started by joking and laughing with him. The teacher positioned herself to the side of Zac and well away from his sight line. Zac was able to focus on his friend and the therapist when he spoke. He presented well and was able to control his stammer for most of the talk.

Zac was awarded a B for this component of his English GCSE.

Talking to authority figures

Individuals who stammer report having more difficulty talking to some people than others: there are some individuals who, because of the position they hold in an organisation and what they represent, can create an increase in communication demand for a person who stammers.

However, it may be that it is not the person themselves who creates the demand but the situation in which the pupil is required to speak to them. For example, a pupil may have to account for their behaviour or performance in front of a senior member of school staff. In such a scenario he will feel challenged and put under pressure. This would be the case whoever he was speaking to.

In such a dialogue, the senior member of staff should not assume guilt or misdemeanour on the basis of a poor level of fluency. The pupil will stammer due to the nature of the communication demand.

Teasing/bullying

Unfortunately stammering is often portrayed and reacted to inappropriately in films, literature and the media (although this seems to have decreased following the release of the film *The King's Speech*). Nevertheless, teasing or bullying are frequently reported by children and young people who stammer. A survey of adults who stammer carried out by the British Stammering Association revealed 82 per cent had experienced bullying in school. Episodes include name calling, imitation or mimicry, making jokes about stammering, and negative reactions to stammering incidents.

This is an area that schools take very seriously. However, it is not always easy to ascertain if a pupil is being bullied or teased. Some pupils will talk about it openly and report incidents immediately. Older individuals are perhaps less likely to adopt an open approach for fear of making the situation worse.

If a pupil does report incidents to a teacher, it is important to find out the following.

- How significant is the problem? Of course it is significant for the individual but the teacher will need to know if it is a one off or whether there have been repeated episodes.
- Who is involved? Is there one particular person or does it involve a group of several pupils?
- Where does it happen? Very often bullying happens in situations in which there is little adult presence. Examples include while entering or leaving school, at break and dinner times, and in changing rooms, cloakrooms or locker rooms.
- Is the teasing or bullying specific to stammering or does it relate to other issues?
- Is the pupil involved in bullying himself and is the incident he has experienced actually a response to that behaviour?

Because bullying often happens out of sight of teachers, it can be difficult for staff to manage. A year or form tutor can work on acceptance of difference for all pupils, as discussed earlier in this chapter. In addition, there are a number of other options.

- Help the young person to develop his self-confidence and self-esteem. When a pupil feels good about himself he is less likely to be affected by the comments of others. Teachers can do much to promote a pupil's feelings of self-worth through the use of praise and encouragement.
- Help the pupil develop coping strategies, for example making up suitable rebuffs to teasing comments about stammering. If a pupil is mimicked in a particular way, he might correct the mimicker by saying: 'Can't you get it right? I said N-N-N-N-N-Newcastle, not Nu-Nu-Nu-Newcastle.' Individuals are often able to come

up with powerful comments to silence the bully. If appropriate, a teacher may help the pupil develop effective behaviour and responses by role playing scenarios with him and providing appropriate feedback. Reardon-Reeves and Yaruss (2013) in *School-Age Stuttering Therapy: A Practical Guide* suggest a number of responses that could be used to deflect the bully:

o   Agree with the bully – *'Yes, I have a stammer'*
o   Ask a question – *'Did you think of that by yourself?'*
o   Reflect the tease comment – *'Why would you want to say something like that to me?'*
o   Use an 'I' message – *'I don't want you to talk to me like that'*
o   Respond to it as if it were a compliment – *'Thanks for noticing that about me'*
o   Walk away with purpose – *'I don't need this'*
o   Say something that is hard for the bully to respond to – *'So . . .?'* or *'And . . .?'*
o   Compliment the bully – *'Yes, I have a stammer. I wish I could talk like you'*
o   Use humour – *'Yes, I stammer. That means everything I say is important enough to say twice!'* or *'Oh, you seem to have caught my stammer.'*

• Help the individual become more integrated into his peer group. This might be achieved through a buddy system for younger pupils or perhaps by encouraging him to join groups, such as sport, drama, music or other school-run clubs.

Key points to remember

In secondary school, management of stammering will consist of helping the pupil to:

• reduce his sensitivity to stammering
• reduce struggle behaviours
• reduce his negative thoughts and feelings
• reduce his avoidance behaviours
• develop an attitude of openness to stammering
• develop useful fluency controlling strategies
• minimise any effect stammering has on his construction of himself, his confidence and self-esteem
• implement the management programme across a range of difficult situations.

The school environment needs to be a safe place to stammer including where the pupil can:

• openly discuss stammering
• risk stammering without fear of ridicule.

The teacher needs to adopt a communication style that facilitates an optimal level of fluency in the young person. This includes:

• using calm, unhurried speech
• using active listening
• demonstrating tolerance and acceptance of verbal responses

- establishing a supportive dialogue with the young person
- supporting the development of his communication, fluency and social skills
- helping him manage any speaking anxiety
- identifying any avoidance behaviours
- helping him develop confidence and positive self-esteem
- establishing a support network for him in school.

The school needs to be aware of specific situations that can be challenging for a pupil who stammers. Situations requiring consideration are:

- registration
- standing in queues
- making verbal contributions in class, including asking questions, reading aloud and giving a presentation
- oral examinations
- talking to authority figures
- incidents of teasing or bullying.

Top tips: How to help a secondary school pupil who stammers

- Create a safe place to stammer.
- Encourage an openness about stammering, including stammering openly and talking about stammering with others.
- Do not rush your speech when talking to the pupil and avoid interrupting him or filling in his words.
- Keep eye contact with him, especially when he is stammering, and maintain a relaxed body posture.
- Establish a supportive dialogue, encouraging the pupil to discuss his thoughts and feelings about stammering and any difficult situations he may be experiencing.
- Develop his general communication skills, i.e. eye contact, body language, appropriate turn taking.
- Be on the lookout for avoidance behaviours.
- Promote confidence and self-esteem.
- Establish a support network.

---

8 Speech and language therapy

This chapter explains how a speech and language therapist might work with a child who stammers and how she might liaise with school staff.

Referrals

Speech and language therapy services have an open referral system. This means that referrals can be received from parents, an adolescent himself or any professional working with the individual. This can include any staff from nursery, primary and secondary schools or further education establishments. Most frequently referrals are received from GPs and family members.

Waiting times can vary but generally there may be up to an eight-week wait. Younger children who are dysfluent are usually prioritised over children with other speech problems. This follows research that has shown early intervention with children who stammer to be most effective.

Speech and language assessment

The assessment process may involve more than one session. At its conclusion, the speech and language therapist will write a report summarising her findings. A specialist therapist is likely to include a specific diagnosis relating to the stammer, for example any underlying auditory processing problems or word-finding issues, the impact of bilingualism, or identification of cluttering, a less common form of dysfluency. This report will be made available to the parents, the GP, the preschool setting/primary or secondary school, and the referring agent.

Speech assessment

A younger child will have a number of assessments of his speaking. These will include reading, monologue and conversation tasks. During these tasks the speech and language therapist will be able to identify the type, frequency and severity of the stammering and any possible impact on his rate of speech.

In addition, she will assess the child's language skills – his understanding of language, use of grammar, vocabulary, word-finding ability, speech sound production and use of language to engage others. These skills will be compared with his developmental profile to ensure that they are commensurate with his developmental age.

Thoughts and feelings

All ages of children and adolescents will be asked how they feel about their speech and their stammer. For a preschool and younger school-aged child this will be done sensitively and with a degree of caution. For example, a therapist may engage the child in a conversation about talking in general and explore any concerns he has without necessarily mentioning stammering unless the child himself gives it a name.

For an older pupil a more direct approach is often possible: does he think there is a problem? If so, what is it, and when and where does it happen? Is he concerned? Does he know why he is talking to the therapist?

Therapists have a range of tools at their disposal to enable them to get the most out of an individual. For more reluctant communicators, including an adolescent who is uncomfortable addressing his stammer, she may use drawing or art therapy and have the individual draw a representation of his stammer. This can prove illuminating and provide a way into a deeper conversation about the person's experiences.

> At the age of 12 Alfie attended a review appointment with his father. The aim of the session was to establish whether or not there were any ongoing concerns with his speech and his stammer.
>
> His father led the conversation and told the speech and language therapist that all was going well. He said Alfie appeared happy and was doing well at school. School had not mentioned any issues and he had good reports at the last parents' evening regarding Alfie's engagement in class and his academic progress.
>
> Alfie sat quietly and appeared to agree with his father's comments. The therapist asked Alfie some direct questions about his talking but was unable to get any elaborate response regarding his thoughts and feelings about his speech.
>
> The therapist then asked Alfie to draw a representation of his stammer. The resulting drawing indicated clearly that he was upset by his stammer and feeling concerned about it. Alfie's drawing was of a frightening man – the kind of image you might see in a horror story or film. He had a hook for one arm. His face and torso were scarred and carried open wounds. His face was snarling, with saliva dribbling from his mouth.
>
> The therapist was then able to talk to Alfie about what the picture meant and how it reflected his feelings about his talking. As a result of the conversation, Alfie attended therapy and met some other young people his own age who stammered but who had more positive feelings about their speech.

The role of parents

Children and adolescents who stammer usually attend a speech and language assessment with their parents. The therapist will interview the parents to establish the history of the stammering, its variability, any significant environmental factors, and any psychological issues related to the demands and capacity model discussed in Chapter 2.

For younger children the speech and language therapist will also be interested in how the family communicate as a group. She may observe them carrying out an interactive task or game together. Her observations will include the family's communication skills, such as turn taking and listening, and how the family manage episodes of dysfluency the child experiences.

Older pupils

An adolescent attending an assessment will usually be seen without his parents to allow him to be open about his thoughts and feelings about stammering and difficult situations. (Parents may have a separate conversation with the therapist or may be included in a joint discussion after the therapist has seen the teenager.) The individual will be encouraged to take responsibility for decisions about the management of his speech, including the types of therapy approaches that might be appropriate.

Therapy

As a starting point to therapy, most speech and language therapists will give parents and young people information about communication skills and stammering in particular. They will feed back the results of their assessments and discuss the various options appropriate to the management of the stammer.

The therapist will be keen to establish a tailor-made management programme for the individual and the family, one that fits with the stammer but more importantly is relevant to the child or young person and their context or speaking environment.

Preschool

Many speech and language therapists working with preschool children will use the 'least first' model identified previously in this book, i.e. only doing what is needed to make a difference. In the first instance this is likely to involve a more indirect approach. The therapist may use the demands and capacities model with the family to identify areas that can be modified to reduce the demands on the child's communication. This might include improved turn taking in the family, use of a slower speech rate when talking to the child, or work on praise to increase his self-esteem.

She will also work on increasing the child's capacities to create the 'balance' that will promote fluency. For example, the child may be given oro-motor exercises to improve the speed and coordination of his articulators. He could be helped to develop expressive language, word finding or rhythm skills. Changes in either the demands or the development of the child's capacities will be introduced incrementally. and the child's speech reviewed regularly to see which change, if any, is making the desired difference.

For some children approaching or entering primary school, where these changes have not resulted in the desired outcome, a more direct approach is sometimes used. This would also be appropriate for children who appear to be at more significant risk of persistent stammering, for example those with a history of stammering in the family, children showing the features of persistent stammering at this early age (struggle behaviours, blocking, multiple repetitions etc. as discussed in Chapter 2) and others whose pattern of stammering indicates an unchanging or increasing level of dysfluency.

The Lidcombe Programme is a direct intervention that is often used with young children of this age. It is a parental programme in which the parent is trained by the therapist to frequently praise fluent speech and *occasionally* comment on stammering incidents, inviting the child to repeat and correct their speech. The parental sessions with the child take place in the home using toys and games that the child chooses. Once the desired level of fluency has been attained and maintained, the programme becomes less structured and the praise and 'correction/comments' are integrated into more everyday speaking situations. The speech and language therapists will review the parents' interaction, the progress of the child and the child's level of fluency. In the early stages these reviews occur on a weekly basis, but in the latter stages of the programme the reviews become less frequent.

Primary school

Some of the early types of intervention used in preschool contexts may extend into primary school years. For other children a change in approach may be needed. In these instances a speech and language therapist may move to a more direct approach.

The aims of therapy at this point are:

- to help the child develop effective communication skills (i.e. non-verbal and verbal behaviours)
- to help the child and family understand stammering in the context of their home life
- to help the child and family identify the 'triggers' that increase or decrease the level of dysfluency, and subsequently to use more of the latter
- to minimise the impact and development of stammering in the child's life, including prevention of avoidance behaviours and management of any negative thoughts and feelings
- to help the child develop and maintain a good level of confidence and self-esteem generally, and with specific regard to communication
- to introduce strategies to help the child enhance his fluency and modify his stammer as appropriate and to gradually use these in everyday situations.

Therapy at this age will usually involve individual sessions with the therapist in clinic or in school. However, some aspects of the management programme will be better suited to a group setting, for example teaching specific fluency strategies or using them in more natural situations. A therapist may be limited in the communication demand she is able to achieve in an individual session with a child. However, using a group of children will increase the turn taking demand, may impact on the speed of delivery, and be more akin to a classroom or other school setting. Groups also reduce the child's feeling of difference and can help normalise the issues.

Secondary school

For secondary school-aged pupils, therapy is almost always directed at changing aspects of speech and, more importantly at this age, managing any negative thoughts or feelings. The approach of the therapist will be to enable the individual to direct his own therapy, taking responsibility for the choices he makes.

The aims of therapy at this point are:

- to help the individual identify the features of his stammer, both overt (above the waterline) and covert (below the waterline) aspects
- to enable the individual to feel less sensitive about his stammer, adopting a more open approach both to the stammer itself and about stammering with other people
- to help the young person manage any avoidance behaviours, including word and situation avoidance and behaviours that compromise his social interaction
- to introduce strategies to help enhance his fluency and modify his stammer as appropriate, and to gradually use these in everyday situations
- to help the young person maintain good communication skills (i.e. non-verbal and verbal behaviours) and improve his social skills
- to help the pupil maintain a good level of confidence and self-esteem generally, and with specific regard to communication
- to help the individual manage the 'triggers' for his stammer, including using fluency strategies and/or developing openness with others about his stammer.

The therapist may use some psychological techniques at this stage. For example, many therapists who specialise in the treatment of stammering are trained in the use of cognitive behavioural therapy, personal construct therapy and/or solution-focused brief therapy.

Therapy for this age often involves group work. This uses the power of peers to effect and maintain change. Groups often run in the school holidays. In some centres in the UK (e.g. Leeds and Swindon) there are groups that combine outdoor activities with speech and language therapy, and these have had very good results.

Liaison visits

Speech and language therapists working with individuals who stammer recognise the importance of collaborating with school staff. The child or young person spends so much time at school that it would be foolish to think a therapist can effect change without considering this part of his life. In addition, it is clear that teachers play an important role in the life of an individual who stammers. A therapist can engage with the teacher and seek to learn from her what is working and what needs to change.

A therapist working from a community clinic or a specialist therapist will wish to visit and talk to a class teacher, the SENCO or a year tutor on a number of occasions. These will be at different points in the child's treatment programme and be for different reasons.

Assessment visits

One of the first occasions a therapist may ask to visit school is as part of her assessment process. It may be that she has been unable to find out the true extent of the child's difficulties and/or specific school-related issues have been mentioned that need further investigation.

The child

The therapist will be interested in seeing how the child communicates in a range of school situations. As a result she may ask to stay for a morning or an afternoon session in order to observe a number of activities, e.g. register, reading aloud, group discussion and/or asking/answering questions in front of the class. She will be comparing how her assessment of the child in clinic compares with how he manages the demands of speaking in school. An example of a speech and language therapist's observational visit checklist (adapted from Stewart and Turnbull's *Working with Dysfluent Children*, 2007) is given in the box.

Checklist for speech and language therapist observing child in class

Entering the class

- How does the child talk with others?
- How does he greet the teacher and his peers?

Registration

- Can the child respond appropriately?
- Is he dysfluent and if so how do both he and his peers respond?

Participation

- Does the child speak spontaneously?
- Does he need prompting to speak?
- Does the class have good turn taking?

Friendships

- Is the child involved in the group or is he a loner?
- How does he get attentions from his peers?

Ability

- How does he cope with the work he is set in class?
- Is he able to concentrate?
- Does he distract others?

Coping with difficulties

- Does he ask questions of peers/the teacher to clarify his understanding?

The teacher

The speech and language therapist will be keen to meet as many members of staff who talk with the child regularly as possible. Sometimes it is not possible to release several members of staff simultaneously so the most significant members of staff, such as the class teacher, year tutor or special needs coordinator, are chosen. The therapist will usually provide the teacher with information about stammering, including appropriate resources.

With regard to the teacher and her teaching style, the therapist will be interested to observe and discuss with her aspects of teaching that are known to create demands on fluency. Topics of interest may include:

- how the teacher understands the dysfluency
- how the teacher currently deals with the child's speech and episodes of dysfluency that occur, both with her in conversation and in classroom interactions
- how she thinks the pupil construes his dysfluency in the class, including examples of avoidance behaviours and negative thoughts and feelings
- how the teacher thinks peers react to his stammer, including examples of acceptance or teasing and bullying behaviour.

She will be keen to observe the teacher's speaking and teaching style and identify any factors that could impact on the child's fluency, i.e. fast speaking rate, use of direct questions, quick-fire responses, use of preparation time in verbal activities.

The speech and language therapist will be aware that the teacher will have the opportunity to observe the pupil's speaking on a daily basis, so she will be keen to use the teacher's eyes and ears as a way of monitoring the effectiveness of the therapy as it progresses over time. She may ask the teacher to observe specific areas of communication and report any significant changes to her.

An example of areas for discussion between a teacher and therapist is provided in the box.

Areas for discussion between speech and language therapist and teacher

- Registration – format of response, time available, attention on child while responding.
- Classroom communication – atmosphere, listening, turn taking, opportunity to discuss personal issues with teachers.
- Teaching style (teachers and other adults playing a role in class) – speed of speech, asking questions.
- Reading aloud – how it is carried out, whether the child is more dysfluent in reading (indicating the child may be using word avoidance strategies in spontaneous speech).
- Assessments – management of oral tests and examinations, need for reasonable adjustments.

General update visits

A therapist will ask to visit the school and meet with the teacher to discuss new information she has about the child or young person. This may be the result of an assessment that she has recently completed. Alternatively it may come about as a result of significant changes in the presentation of the stammer and/or changes in his treatment that could impact on his speaking in school. The therapist will discuss this information with the teacher and determine how this might affect and change the management of the pupil's stammer in school. For example, a child may have learnt a new fluency strategy and be ready to use it in more demanding situations, such as answering questions in class. The therapist will discuss the rationale for the treatment, how the teacher can talk to the pupil about his level of competency and how best to support him in using this newly acquired skill.

Alternatively a child may be about to embark on a series of regular therapy sessions. In this instance the therapist will be keen to find out from the teacher the best times when the pupil can be absent. She will also talk about how he can be integrated back into the class and how he could answer any questions from his peers about to his absence. (Many children who have not yet developed an open approach to stammering will not wish others to know about their therapy sessions.)

Older pupils may be given the option of attending the meeting themselves but, even if they choose not to be there, they will be involved in determining what is discussed at any meeting.

Openness

If the pupil is working on developing an open approach to his stammer, this may also necessitate a school visit by the therapist. Openly stammering when you have tried to hide it for a number of years is a big step for anyone to take. As such the therapist will be anxious to make the teacher aware of this approach, and to assure her that the episodes of open stammering are not a deterioration in the pupil's speech but a development of a more open and relaxed approach to stammering. The therapist will help the teacher in creating an environment that enables the pupil to work on this area.

Another way in which the pupil might work on openness is to talk to others about stammering in general and his stammer in particular. The therapist will be able to advise the teacher on developing open conversations with the pupil. In addition there may be an opportunity for him to do a presentation on stammering within the school curriculum. Alternatively the therapist could discuss with the teacher how a presentation might fit within an appropriate context.

On occasions a speech and language therapist may suggest to the teacher that she come and give a short presentation to the class about stammering. This suggestion usually has its origins in discussions held between the individual who stammers and the therapist. It would be part of the openness process but may be an intermediary step to enable the pupil to discuss the issue of stammering with his peers.

Transition to secondary

Sometimes in the course of a therapy session a pupil will discuss with his therapist concerns he has regarding the transition from primary to secondary school. This can be a very significant move for the child and one that comes with many pre-emptions and anticipations.

For a child who stammers these concerns can centre on his speech and worries about particular situations that would not be problematic for a fluent speaker. It is important that these issues are addressed before the pupil starts his new school, so the speech and language therapist will agree with the child what is to be discussed and then visit the school to talk to the teaching staff. The child (and his parents) will be encouraged to attend the meeting, which usually takes place in the summer term before he starts secondary school.

Usually at this meeting strategies for managing difficult situations can be discussed and the beginnings of a support network established, for example having a named person who the pupil can go to in the first instance if there are issues with his speech or who can seek him out from time to time to check everything is going well.

Oral assessments

A further reason for a speech and language therapist to visit school is to discuss any oral assessments and any reasonable adjustments that might be made for a pupil who stammers. She will be able to provide evidence, including a specialised report, that the school can use when applying for adjustment to the examination.

She can also advise on ways in which the demands of the examination can be modified within the criteria of the assessment. For example, the audience size and the time allowed can be factors that can be changed for an English oral assessment.

On the day of an examination she might also see the individual in school prior to his presentation and revise any specific strategies that help his speech.

Workshops for teachers

Training sessions for teachers who encounter pupils who stammer in their school or class are of course a good idea. However, for teachers the practicalities of having time off to attend a session often make it difficult.

Speech and language therapists can be asked to provide training to a school as part of their annual school training programme. Alternatively, specialist therapists often run courses for teachers on a regular basis. With sufficient warning a teacher may be able to arrange cover and attend these typically two-hour sessions. They can then cascade the information to the rest of their team and/or relevant school staff.

A typical training session will include:

* general information about stammering as a speech disorder
* a description of the components of a stammer
* the development of stammering in children
* the impact of stammering in relation to school life
* difficult situations encountered by pupils who stammer
* strategies to manage stammering in school, especially the difficult situations.

Due to the busy schedules of teachers and therapists, liaison is often not the priority it should be. However, there is no doubt that everyone benefits when these conversations take place. The pupil is able to have a holistic plan that is tailored to the important parts of his daily life. The teacher is better informed about stammering in general, and specifically about the individual's stammer. The therapist has an ally in monitoring the effectiveness of her therapy programme: everyone is 'on task' and talking to each other about the progress of the plan, which can only be to the benefit of the pupil.

9 Final words

The last words come from the children themselves. There have been several examples of groups of children who stammer giving advice to adults about how best to help. In a project carried out by the Michael Palin Centre, children were asked how they would like to be helped. Their comments included the following.

Give us time to think and speak

'A good teacher doesn't interrupt what I'm saying. They give me time to speak.'

'After I've been asked a question, if I was given the time to start thinking about the answer and my speech as well it would be very helpful because I could think of some techniques for my speech.'

Let us finish our sentences in our own time

'People in general will try and finish your sentences for you. They probably think that it helps, but the majority of people with stammer would rather know that they can finish their own sentences.'

Tell us we're doing OK and calm us down if needed, but don't advise us about our speech

'I don't really like being told to slow down.'

'People tell me to hurry up, but I get annoyed because I speed up and then I stammer more, so then it takes even more time to get the words out.'

British Stammering Association advice

The British Stammering Association reported on a group of children who met for some fluency workshops. They compiled the following advice to share with their teachers.

Do – treat us like everyone else in the school
Do – ask us what helps us to speak more fluently (it can vary)
Do – ask how much we want to contribute in class assembly and concerts
Do – be positive and make eye contact
Do – give us time to express ourselves

Do not – rush us – give us time to finish
Do not – finish off words/sentences for us
Do not – answer for us
Do not – interrupt when we are trying
Do not – tease/mimic us
Do – tell others not to tease us/mimic us
Do – share this information with others

References and resources

References

Crowe, TA & Walton, JH (1981). 'Teachers' attitudes toward stuttering.' *Journal of Fluency Disorders*, 6, 163–174.

Reardon-Reeves, N & Yaruss, JS (2013). *School-Age Stuttering Therapy: A Practical Guide*. Stuttering Therapy Resources, Texas.

Stewart, T & Turnbull, J (2007). *Working with Dysfluent Children: Practical Approaches to Assessment and Therapy*. Speechmark Publishing, Brackley.

Resources

For teachers

- **The School-Age Child Who Stutters: Working Effectively with Attitudes and Emotions – A Workbook, by Kristin A. Chmela and Nina Reardon**. 2001, Stuttering Foundation of America. Lots of ideas for working with school-age children.
- **Stammering: Advice for All Ages, by Renée Byrne and Louise Wright**. 2008, Sheldon Press. Aimed at both adults who stammer and parents of children who stammer, the book includes information about stammering, details of therapeutic approaches, advice, exercises and contributions from people who stammer.
- **Coping with Stammering, by Trudy Stewart and Jackie Turnbull**. 1997, Sheldon Press. Written by two specialist speech and language therapists, this is a self-help book for anyone who has a stammer, and who has questions and concerns about stammering.
- **Young Children Who Stutter (Ages 2–6), by J. Scott Yaruss and Nina A. Reardon-Reeves**. 2007 (5th edition), National Stuttering Association. This book is designed to help parents of children who stammer. It contains much useful information about stammering and looks at the best treatment options for a child of this age.
- **Working with Dysfluent Children: Practical Approaches to Assessment and Therapy, by Trudy Stewart and Jackie Turnbull**. 2007, Speechmark. This expanded and revised edition analyses dysfluency in children and provides the reader with practical ways of handling such difficulties in collaboration with the child, parents and carers.
- **The Treatment of Stuttering in the Young School-Aged Child, edited by Roberta Lees and Cameron Stark**. 2005, Wiley. Primarily for students and clinicians working with children who stutter aged 7–12, it describes a number of different

treatments. The contributors also discuss theoretical models on which these are based and ways of measuring outcomes.

- *Fifty Great Activities for Children Who Stutter*, **by Peter Reitzes**. 2006. Pro-Ed. Intended for children between 7 and 12, this book contains a large collection of insights and ideas for therapy success, together with 50 possible activities for young stutterers.
- *Can I Tell You about Stammering?* **by Sue Cottrell**. 2013, Jessica Kingsley. A guide for friends, family and professionals. Available to buy at www.jkp.com/catalogue/book/9781849054157
- *Voice Unearthed*, **by Doreen Holte**. 2011, Holte. Written by a parent of a child who stammers, this is a challenging read for parents and professionals working with children who stammer.

CD ROMs

The following are all published by the British Stammering Association, with updated versions available online (www.stammeringineducation.net).

- *A Guide to Good Practice when Working with Pupils Who Stammer in Primary Schools*
- *A Guide to Good Practice when Working with Pupils Who Stammer in Secondary Schools*
- *A Guide to Good Practice when Working with Pupils Who Stammer in Primary Schools: Scottish Primary School Version*
- *A Guide to Good Practice when Working with Pupils Who Stammer in Secondary Schools: Scottish Secondary School Version*

DVDs

- *Wait, Wait, I'm Not Finished Yet*, **by the Michael Palin Centre**. 2009. This DVD, featuring two films of children who stammer (longer and shorter versions), is intended to raise awareness across the educational world about the problems in school of children and young people who stammer.
- *Stuttering: Straight Talk for Teachers*, **by Kristin Chmela and Bill Murphy**. 2009 (3rd edition), Stuttering Foundation of America. Students who stutter talk to teachers about their experiences. The authors answer questions and offer expert advice about what works in the classroom. You can also watch the video online on the SFA website: www.stutteringhelp.org/stuttering-straight-talk-teachers

For children

- *Hooray for Aiden*, **by Karen Hollett**. 2010, Hooray Publishing. Aimed at children aged 4–9, this book tells the story of a little girl called Aiden who moves to a new school in a new town. Slowly, with a little help from a teacher, Aiden learns that it's OK to stutter.
- *Sometimes I Just Stutter*, **by Eelco de Gues**. Stuttering Foundation of America. A book for children between ages 7 and 12. Highly recommended because of the easy way it is written, including letters from children who stammer, and illustrations.

- ***Stuttering is Cool: A Guide to Stuttering in a Fast-Talking World*, by Daniele Rossi**. Suitable for those aged 10+ but the author notes that it is more suited to adult/older teens. It is available to buy online at www.stutteringiscool.com/book
- ***Who-Who-Who Goes Hoo-Hoo-Hoo?* by Peter Scheider and Gisela Schartmann**. 2012, Speechmark. This children's book tells the story of a hedgehog who stammers. He feels lonely till he meets a mouse who stammers and together they save the forest animals from a dangerous monster. Suitable for young children and their friends.
- ***Steggie's Stammer*, by Jack Hughes**. 2012, Wayland. This book describes how Steggie, a little female dinosaur with a stammer, rescues her friends when they all get lost in the Dark Forest.
- ***The Golden Bird*, by Berlie Doherty**. 1998, Mammoth. An uplifting child's story, beautifully illustrated.

DVD

- ***Stuttering: For Kids, By Kids***. 2004, Stuttering Foundation of America. Swish and his young friends talk about stuttering, teasing, what helps and how to teach others about stuttering. Features cartoon animation and real children in an engaging and lively video. You can also watch the video online on the SFA website: www.stutteringhelp.org/content/stuttering-kids-kids

For teens

- ***Do You Stutter? A Guide for Teens*, edited by Jane Fraser and William Perkins**. Speech Foundation of America. A self-help book with individual chapters written by specialist American speech and language pathologists who themselves stammer. Is accompanied by the DVD listed below.

DVD

- ***Stuttering: Straight Talk for Teens***. 2010, Stuttering Foundation of America. This 30-minute DVD is narrated by American high school students who stammer, and provides good advice both on the general nature of stammering and the problems faced by secondary school students. Accompanies the book listed above. You can also watch the video online on the SFA website: www.stutteringhelp.org/content/stuttering-straight-talk-teens

Useful resources/advice agencies

British Stammering Association

15 Old Ford Road
Bethnal Green
London E2 9PJ
Telephone: 0845 603 2001
Email: info@stammering.org

Education hotline: 01606 77374
Education email: education@stammering.org

Royal College of Speech & Language Therapists

2 White Hart Yard
London SE1 1NX
Telephone: 020 7378 1200

Stuttering Foundation of America

PO Box 11749
Memphis, TN 38111-0749
Telephone: (800) 992-9392 or (901) 761-0343
Email: info@stutteringhelp.org

Index

Note: *italics* denote figures.